MW00561282

Get on Board

Praise for *Get on Board: Earning Your Ticket to a Corporate Board Seat*

"If there is any book to read, this is a 'must read' for anyone who wants to serve on a corporate board but does not know where to start. Olga V. Mack sums it all up through insights and practical advice on becoming a corporate director."
—Caroline Tsay, CEO, Compute Software and Corporate Director at The Coca-Cola Company and Morningstar

"A 'must-read' book for everyone who wants to serve on a corporate board but does not know where to start."
—Alison Davis, Cofounder, Fifth Era and Corporate Board Director at Fiserv, Ooma, RBS, Unisys

"Don't just dream of sitting on a corporate board. Read *Get on Board: Earning Your Ticket to a Corporate Board Seat*. Work and learn how to become the agent of change you want to see in the corporate world."
—Adam R. Sand, CEO, Shopkick

"Olga V. Mack has helped pave the road for more people to serve on corporate boards, and in her new book, *Get on Board: Earning Your Ticket to a Corporate Board Seat*, Olga provides a practical 'how to' on becoming a corporate director. It's a 'must read' for all future directors."
—Janine Yancey, Founder & CEO, Emtrain

"If you think joining a corporate board is for a select few, think again. In *Get on Board: Earning Your Ticket to a Corporate Board Seat*, Olga V. Mack shares the practical strategies to become a corporate director."
—Denise Brosseau, CEO, Thought Leadership Lab, and author, Ready to Be a Thought Leader?

"Olga V. Mack has hit it out of the park with this great book about securing a board position. She nails it. There is so much great information that will help you navigate the corporate board process."
—Marlene Williamson, CEO and Board Director, Watermark, and Board Director, VibeChain, Inc.

"In the age of disruption, rapid technological advancement, and lack of trust, there is a growing need for authentic leadership at every level of the company. This is especially true at the corporate board level. Olga V. Mack's new book demystifies corporate board service for all leaders and gives them information and tools to step up and restore trust in the corporate world."
—Coco Brown, CEO and Founder, The Athena Alliance

"*Get on Board* is a 'must read' for any person who strives to grow a company or career by claiming a seat in the room where it happens."
—Sarah Feingold, former General Counsel of Etsy and Vroom

"*Get on Board: Earning Your Ticket to a Corporate Board Seat* is propelling the success of the California legislative action requiring women on corporate boards by providing the framework and self-efficacy women require to enter through the doors that have been closed to women."
—Julie Abrams, CEO, How Women Lead and Board Leaders

Get on Board

Earning Your Ticket to a Corporate Board Seat

Olga V. Mack

Editor and Contributor
Nancy E. Sheppard

 BUSINESS EXPERT PRESS

Get on Board: Earning Your Ticket to a Corporate Board Seat
Copyright © Business Expert Press, LLC, 2019.

All rights reserved. No part of this publication may be reproduced, stored in a retrieval system, or transmitted in any form or by any means— electronic, mechanical, photocopy, recording, or any other except for brief quotations, not to exceed 250 words, without the prior permission of the publisher.

First published in 2019 by
Business Expert Press, LLC
222 East 46th Street, New York, NY 10017
www.businessexpertpress.com

ISBN-13: 978-1-94999-140-6 (paperback)
ISBN-13: 978-1-94999-141-3 (e-book)

Business Expert Press Entrepreneurship and Small Business Management Collection

Collection ISSN: 1946-5653 (print)
Collection ISSN: 1946-5661 (electronic)

Cover image by Flamingo Images/Shutterstock.com
Cover and interior design by S4Carlisle Publishing Services Private Ltd., Chennai, India

First edition: 2019

10 9 8 7 6 5 4 3 2 1

Printed in the United States of America.

Dedication

For mom, the strongest and most generous woman.
She always believes in me.

Abstract

Directors, chairpersons, chief executive officers (CEOs), recruiters, and other professionals who assist boards all reveal that becoming a director is a journey. The process can take one to five years. It involves a lot of educating, networking, and strategic positioning. In other words, just like everything worth pursuing, it mostly involves a lot of hard work! Yes, there are occasional glimpses of luck. But there are definitely no "magical" moments, invisible hands, or other miracles.

This book is a practical beginner's guide for anyone considering becoming a director, from young professionals seeking board service in the future to seasoned professionals contemplating an imminent career change. This book answers the most common questions about board service and demystifies the board journey process. It also provides examples of successful director biographies and resumes. Finally, it shares actionable strategies and helpful worksheets that you can use today to start your board service. After reading this book, any professional will be convinced that corporate board service is within their reach—and will be ready to pursue it!

Keywords

corporate boards; boards; corporate governance; governance; corporate director; director; executive; management; strategy; career; leadership; business; business & finance; business leadership; business management; business mentoring; business coaching

Contents

Acknowledgments

With the deepest gratitude, I wish to thank all people who inspired, supported, or illuminated me through their presence, words, or assistance in my board advocacy, teaching, and writing adventures. This has been a fun, enlightening, impactful, educational, and rewarding journey. And I am forever grateful for the opportunity.

Nancy Sheppard, who contributed to this book, her wise words, and sound advice have made a difference in the lives of many professionals, including mine. Thank you for all your support and encouragements!

Vitaliy, my dad, who has taught me that I am limited by my imagination only. He believed in me long before I learned to believe in myself. Thank you for teaching me never to settle. I miss you every day!

Irina, my mom, who is always there for me, selflessly and without any reservations. Full of love, loyalty, and passion, she is the strongest woman I know. Thank you for your daily unconditional love!

Kevin, my husband, whose consistent affection and support make me feel like the luckiest woman on the planet. You are my best friend and the love of my life. Thank you for the adventure!

And, finally, to my daughters, Katie and Natalie. To Katie, whose views are enlightened beyond her years, and to Natalie, whose persistence, will, and determination are second to none. My daughters are precious. And their presence inspires me to aim higher every day. Thank you for the opportunity to guide you!

Olga V. Mack
April 30, 2019
Dublin, California

Introduction

A few years ago, I started the Women Serve on Boards movement. Our goal was simple: pressure the remaining Fortune 500 companies with all-male boards to elect or appoint their first woman directors. Two petitions, a few letters, and countless social media posts later, we convinced some Fortune 500 companies to hire their first women to serve on their boards of directors.

Then I found myself asking, "How can I scale this cause?" I ultimately concluded that public policy is the answer. So I fiercely advocated, testified, and mobilized support for what became known as California "SB 826," a 2018 California law that requires public companies with their principal executive office in California recruit women onto their corporate boards.

In a process of advocating for this cause, I learned that many professionals—men and women—are pursuing or at least considering board service. I also realized that the process of becoming a director seems mysterious to many professionals. Many imagine that an invisible hand takes a few select professionals and gives them a corporate board seat.

This, of course, is a myth. The reality is much more intentional than magical.

I have spoken with and interviewed many directors, chairpersons, CEOs, recruiters, and other professionals who assist boards. They all reveal that becoming a corporate director is a journey that takes one to five years. It involves a lot of educating, networking, and strategic positioning.

In other words, just like everything worth pursuing, it mostly involves a lot of hard work! Yes, there are occasional glimpses of luck. But there are no "magical" moments, invisible hands, or other miracles.

Throughout my advocacy efforts, many professionals—both supporters and strangers—have approached me with practical questions about boards and board service. Their questions ranged from "Why pursue board service?" to "How can I join a board?"

At first the process of answering questions was exciting, especially because it allowed me to expand my professional network. Over time, however, I found myself answering the same questions many times over.

I realized that no matter how much I would like to, I cannot have lunch, coffee, or even a phone call with everyone who wants to learn more about boards. So I have written down all the questions that I have been repeatedly answering and compiled the answers into this book. This way I can help greater number of professionals.

This book is for professionals of all ages at any stage of their career. It is useful to young professionals, as it suggests what jobs and assignments they need to seek and what skills to develop if they want to pursue board service in the future. It is also useful to professionals who are contemplating becoming a director soon or who have just started their board journeys.

Of course, there are many comprehensive advisors and consultants who can hold your hand and guide you through your journey to becoming a board director. Depending on your goals and resources, you may consider using these means as well. I have listed some of them in Appendix C. Yet, even with guides, the work to gain a director position is still yours, and you must have the skills and experiences and personal gravitas that will take you to this level of leadership.

This book is aimed to be a short and easy read that answers many initial questions, demystifies the process, and shares actionable strategies that you can implement today. The chapters can be read in any order.

My hope is that after reading this book, most professionals will be convinced that corporate board service is within their reach if he or she chooses to pursue it. It is not for a select, highly connected, famous, and wealthy few. And it certainly does not require any "magic."

Clear intention, relevant experience, coherent strategy, time investment, and purposeful execution are all you need to eventually make your director dream a reality.

Have a great corporate board journey, enjoy the ride, and—perhaps most importantly—share your stories, strategies, templates, worksheets, and tips with me at http://olgamack.com/contact/. I may incorporate them in the next edition of this book.

Let us learn and serve on boards together!

CHAPTER 1

Understanding Boards

The board of directors, whether for-profit or nonprofit, oversees the activities of a company and represents its shareholders. The board is directly accountable to the shareholders. Each year the company will hold an annual general meeting (AGM) where the directors report to shareholders on the performance of the company, its future, and its strategies; they may also submit themselves for reelection to the board at the AGM.

Public companies must have a board of directors. Private companies are not required to have boards, although many of them do.

The board of directors' key purpose is to ensure the company's long-term prosperity. Oversight of management, including the hiring, evaluation, and dismissal of the chief executive officer (CEO), is seen as one of the most important duties of a fiduciary board. The board directs the company's affairs by representing the appropriate interests of its shareholders and stakeholders. In addition to business and financial issues, boards deal with numerous other issues such as corporate governance, corporate social responsibility, and corporate ethics.

Boards are an incredibly complex facet of corporate culture. Before pursuing board service, which is a sizable commitment, it is helpful to have a foundational understanding of boards. For example, this chapter discusses what boards do, who appoints directors, time commitments for board service, how much directors get paid, and the factors that influence corporate board composition. It then delves into the board structure, committees, and the role of the chair. Finally, it discusses how to assess your qualifications, how directors stay effective, and whether board placement service is right for you.

What Do the Boards Do?

The board of directors is composed of the key people who make decisions about important issues, hire the CEO, and perform other roles and responsibilities. They are the governing body of a company.

For example, hiring a CEO, making any major acquisition, selling the company, and numerous other key events all require the board's approval. Because the board determines the overall strategy of the company, its members must be engaged, diligent, responsible, and have a high degree of integrity.

The prime function of every director is to help in the effective functioning of the organization, while ensuring no interruptions in the output. Some of the core responsibilities of a director include the following:

- **Guide the CEO and monitor management**

  The core function of a director is to work with the CEO of the company. The board selects the CEO; the board also has the power to remove the CEO. The board evaluates the work of the CEO. The members of the board encourage the CEO to handle situations effectively, aiding him or her to make better decisions. The board assists the CEO and other members of the leadership team. They make key decisions, facilitating introductions, oversight, and inquiries.

  In sum, the board recruits, retains, supervises, compensates, and evaluates the CEO. This is the most prominent function of a board of directors. It is the main reason that only skilled, experienced, and capable candidates are considered to join a board.

  The board also monitors the performance of the management. They keenly observe the activities and the policies followed.

- **Determine company strategy**

  Directors must keep raising questions about the overall strategy that the organization follows. They focus on their advantages and disadvantages. This includes taking care of the company's financial stability, selecting its target market, and designing the present and future of the company. The board is also responsible for creating the organization's vision and goals.

- **Safeguard the values of the organization**
  The board ensures that the company progresses responsibly and effectively. They ensure that all the activities that are taking place in the organization are conducted ethically and legally.

  Boards have numerous other responsibilities:

  - **Controlling and monitoring various functions of the board.** For example, the board is responsible for monitoring the auditing process. The board hires auditors.
  - **Maximizing long-term shareholder returns and protecting the company's assets and investments.** This responsibility applies to the boards of most for-profit companies.
  - **Monitoring internal controls and policies.** The board determines company policies and ensures that internal controls are effective.
  - **Planning.** The board reviews and evaluates present and future opportunities and risks. They consider the geopolitical environment, industry trends, and economic cycles.
  - **Collaborating with the senior management.** The board communicates with the senior management. It must also monitor and evaluate that the management implements policies, strategies, and business plans. It must delegate authority to the management.
  - **Staying accountable to shareholders.** The board exercises accountability to shareholders and ensures that communications both to and from shareholders are effective. They promote the goodwill and support of shareholders and relevant stakeholders.
  - **Acting in good faith.** In the event of a conflict of interest between the company's interests and their own, the directors must disclose and always favor the company. They must act with due skill and care.

Who Appoints Directors?

Shareholders ultimately determine the composition of the board. They may appoint or dismiss directors. The shareholders may also fix the minimum and maximum number of directors, and the size and length of the term. In some circumstances, the board can appoint (but usually not dismiss) a director, as well.

Often, a majority of shareholders may dismiss a director from office; they may need to follow special procedures for this purpose. The procedure is complex, and legal advice will always be required.

Who Is an Independent Director?

An independent director, or outside (nonexecutive) director, is a member of a board who does not work for the company. In contrast, inside directors are members of the corporation, usually part of the corporation's management team.

For example, New York Stock Exchange (NYSE) requires listed companies to "have a majority of independent directors." NYSE listing requirements define outside directors as having no "material relationship" to the company. NYSE listing requirements further explain: "Effective boards of directors exercise independent judgment in carrying out their responsibilities. Requiring a majority of independent directors will increase the quality of board oversight and lessen the possibility of damaging conflicts of interest."

Outside directors contribute to the organization by advising the management on strategy and operations, drawing on their professional experience. They also ensure that executives act in the interest of shareholders.

Independent directors bring diverse backgrounds to decision making. They are also unbiased regarding company decisions.

What Are the Time Commitments to Serve on a Board?

Serving on a board offers many opportunities and responsibilities. However, directors must invest significant time to fulfill their responsibilities. They must prepare and attend board meetings, provide guidance, understand and analyze financial strategy, serve on committees, and fulfill numerous other obligations.

The role of the directors is substantially more complex and often time-consuming. Most boards meet at least four times a year. In some companies, the board meets more often. The board will almost always meet more often if circumstances warrant, such as when a merger or acquisition occurs, or when the board needs to deal with a crisis management event such as a CEO's unexpected departure or news putting the company's reputation at risk. The board survey reports indicate a director must commit a minimum of 60 hours per quarter for public board service, which does not include travel time.

Key time commitments outside of the actual board meeting itself include the following:

- Considering strategies for the development of business
- Monitoring competitors to understand the marketplace
- Keeping an eye on industry trends, the development of the business, and any applicable laws
- Providing guidance to the chairperson, company leadership, and the management team
- Meeting with the professional and financial advisors of the company
- Serving on board committees
- Visiting company facilities
- Understanding company culture
- Attending governance and board training events
- Traveling for formal and informal events

There are numerous other responsibilities a director may have, which can vary based on the organization and board type. If you are joining a board it is important to discuss the time commitments and expectations first. You must make sure that you are ready to meet the expectations and obligations that may come with the job.

How Much Does a Director Get Paid?

The compensation of directors varies depending on industry, experience, company size, and geographies. The number of meetings required and whether the company is public or private often play a role. Compensation also varies across different types of boards—advisory boards, private boards, public boards, nonprofit boards, startup boards, family boards, and others.

Director pay is set up differently in different companies. Most directors receive an annual retainer fee for board meetings. They may also be paid an additional retainer or fee for committee work, and a chair or lead director is usually paid an additional fee. Due to increased risks for director liabilities and the time required for board service, corporations often continue boosting director pay, year after year, often faster than they do for their regular employees.

- **Public boards**

  On public boards, director compensation is generally divided between stock and cash. Compensation is public knowledge and can be found in SEC reports. Most directors receive an allocation of shares from the stock of the company. The trend over the last decade has been away from stock options and toward restricted stock, deferred stock, and outright stock. Only on rare occasions are directors paid by the hour. Per board meeting fees continue to decline as the preferred compensation method with only about 10 percent of the S&P 500 paying meeting attendance fees in 2018 compared to 45 percent a decade ago.

  Most companies require directors to hold the stock grants for a certain number of years. The total compensation for each individual member depends on different factors, such as how long they have been involved with the company, their specific skills or knowledge, whether they have a high public profile, and many other factors.

  Pay increases with company size, averaging at $298,981 in 2018 for directors of the S&P 500 with 56 percent of their pay in stock grants, according to the Spencer Stuart Board Index. A study released in 2017, by Arthur J. Gallagher & Co., showed the total pay for Russell 3000 companies at $191,043 made up of 58 percent equity. According to some calculations, the median pay for a board seat at a micro-cap company (one with less than $500 million in revenues) was a little over $100,000.

  In general, public company boards in the UK and EU pay less than similar size U.S. public company boards and provide more of their compensation in cash. Most corporate codes in Europe recommend against granting nonexecutive directors stock options or similar stock performance-related incentive.

- **Private boards**

  There is a lot of variance in compensation for different types of private boards. The 2019 Private Company Board Comp Survey by Lodestone Global reported that the median total compensation (across 32 countries and 33 industries, with 50 percent family-owned companies) was $41,500 with a $30,000 retainer. A well-established large private board generally offers higher compensation to its pro- spective directors, as it competes with public boards for qualified directors. It is not unusual for a medium-sized private company to offer prospective directors somewhere between $15,000 and $40,000 per year. Some private companies offer compensation like that offered by micro-cap public companies, especially if they have $200 to $500 million in revenue. This comes to around $100,000.

  Family-owned companies often pay outside directors, as other private companies pay their directors, with cash and little to no equity.

  Outside directors of a Private Equity (PE)-owned company are often introduced by the private equity firm that owns the portfolio company. These outside directors are generally paid by the PE fund owner and their compensation is similar to public company board members.

- **Startup boards**

  If you are wondering how startup directors get paid, well, here is the *theory* behind it. Directors receive compensation for their roles in a startup, but there are unique factors that influence the total compensation package. These are normally related to time com- mitment, expertise, experience, knowledge, and other factors.

  It is not unusual for a startup to manage money carefully. So they are often not able to throw a cash compensation at a prospect- ive director! As a result, startup directors are more likely rewarded in the form of equity.

  At the early stage, prospective directors may be looking at up to 1 percent equity, based on time commitment, expertise, experience, knowledge, and other factors. As the company grows and becomes financially stable, equity compensation rates drop and are replaced by cash. So over time as the startup matures, the cash portion of the package increases, and the equity portion diminishes. Even startups that have raised plenty of money often offer an equity-based compensation of around 0.25 to 0.75 percent.

Another major factor affecting the compensation of a startup director is how involved they are with the company. There are three different levels: high, medium, and low engagement levels. Highly engaged members are more involved. They should expect the highest pay among the three categories. Medium engagement-level members lie somewhere between active and semi-active. Their compensation is also moderate. Finally, the lowest compensated are members who are less engaged. They are present and accountable for board meetings and often communicate through calls. They are not less important than the other directors, but their compensation is lower compared to the other two categories.

Although equity and engagement are the two main factors that determine the compensation of a startup director, their compensation also depends on their experience, expertise, and knowledge. Popularity and notoriety of the prospective director in the business world may also affect their compensation.

- **Advisory boards**

  Compensation for advisory board member varies dramatically. It is not unusual for an advisory board member not be compensated or to receive only an equity grant, especially at startups. Some companies pay between $250 and $1,500 for each meeting attended, give stock in the company, or pay members to participate in the annual strategic session for about $5,000. But this is not true for all startups. Therefore, before joining an advisory board it is extremely important to have a very honest discussion about your time commitments and expected compensation.

- **Nonprofit boards**

  Serving on a nonprofit board is typically a volunteer activity. Usually, nonprofit boards do not compensate their directors. Only a small number of nonprofit organizations pay their members.

In fact, many nonprofits expect their directors to make a sizable annual donation or be heavily involved in fundraising efforts. Therefore, before joining a nonprofit board, consider having a very honest discussion about your time commitments and obligations.

How to Assess Qualifications to Serve on the Board?

Professionals who are asked to serve on a board often have significant executive experience or other equivalent professional experience. Here are some questions that you need to ask yourself in order to check whether you are qualified for board service.

- **Am I passionate about this company?**
  This is very important! You need to ask yourself whether you are passionate about helping the company get to its desired heights. Are you interested in the vision and mission of the company? If the answer is "no," you probably do not need to ask any more questions.

- **Am I knowledgeable enough?**
  As a prospective board director, you must be knowledgeable in various aspects of your discipline, industry, and the company. This does not mean that directors are not prone to mistakes or that they know everything. A certain level of knowledge is required to be a qualified candidate.

- **Am I yearning to learn?**
  Serving on a board means you must be open-minded, ask good questions, know how to work with experts, and stay on top of the industry. This means that you must have the mindset to challenge yourself and to learn new concepts and ideas.

- **How do I relate with others?**
  A board comprises more than one director. Each director has valuable knowledge, life experiences, and industry expertise. Can you respectively interact and constructively disagree with them while maintaining good professional relationships? There will be times when you are likely to experience disagreements, whether it be tactical or philosophical ones. How do you handle such situations?

How would you influence the outcome you want to see? Some ask bluntly, "Can you 'check' your ego at the door?" and "Do you have a sense of humor?"

- **Can I serve?**
  Being a director places you in a position where you are serving the company. After all, your goal is to maximize long-term return for the company's shareholders. You need to know whether you can withstand the challenges of the role and serve the company well. This involves time commitment, willingness to learn, and an uncompromising dedication to realizing the company's goals.

The *Board Profile and Competency Matrix* worksheet in Appendix B can help you to identify the experience, knowledge, and skills that you can leverage for board service.

What Factors Generally Influence Board Composition?

Board composition is typically closely related to issues of board independence and the various experiences of outside directors. Companies must balance these competing interests and related trade-offs when they assemble their boards:

- **Status quo vs. new perspective: a very sophisticated balancing act**
  Against the foundation of historic worldwide financial downturns, companies often want to enlist directors with new perspectives who also possess the experience and skills appropriate to address current challenges. There is also a developing appreciation for diverse boards, which are more likely to pose essential inquiries instead of surrendering to "general thinking."

  Boards also need to stay productive and focused, as well as protect and use their current institutional information and connections. They need to have a long-term vision and create a sense of stability for all major stakeholders such as employees, investors, the leadership, the management, the community, and regulators.

- **Structure vs. diversity: trade-offs to consider**

  The boards, especially at more established organizations, have frequently set a standard for choosing directors who can fit effortlessly into existing board culture and will work well with current company directors and the senior leadership. Therefore, CEOs, executives, and directors often rely on their professional or social networks to recruit directors. This tendency often increases board composition homogeneity. Homogeneous boards may be weak and insufficient to meet the needs and wants of diverse clients, partners, employees, suppliers, investors, and other key stakeholders. They may hinder the company's success in an increasingly global economy, shifting political climate, and increasing pace of innovation.

- **Granular proficiency vs. long-term oversight**

  A corporate board oversees its company's direction to maximize the company's long-term returns to its shareholders. They normally do not manage day-to-day operations. However, it is a significant asset for a director to understand the company, its industry, and its historic evolution. In fact, many suggest that it is paramount to the success of a corporate director. Some boards put less emphasis on recruiting directors with specific capabilities related to the company or industry.

How Are the Boards Structured?

Board meetings are held periodically, usually at least quarterly, so that the directors can discharge their responsibility to control the company's overall situation, strategy, and policy, and to monitor the exercise of any delegated authority. There the individual directors can report on their areas of responsibility including the work that they do in the committees.

Normally, there are four primary board committees: executive, audit, compensation, and nominating.

- The executive committee tends to be a smaller group that might meet when the full board is not available.

- The audit committee reviews the financial statements with internal auditors and outside audit companies. It is often made up of independent directors.
- The compensation committee determines the salaries and bonuses of top executives, including the board itself. It is often made up of independent directors.
- The nominations and governance committees decide the slate of directors for the shareholders to vote their approval and provide general oversight of governance of the corporation and board.

Technology, risk, and compliance committees are additional committees that are becoming more prevalent. There may be others, depending on corporate philosophy, culture, history, special circumstances, or a company's line of business.

What Is the Audit Committee? Who Is Qualified to Serve?

The audit committee is an operating committee of the board that supervises the financial reporting and disclosure process of a company. The audit committee members are chosen from the board often by the chairperson of the company.

It is one of the most important committees. It is required for many companies, especially public. For example, a qualifying audit committee is required for a U.S. publicly traded company to be listed on a stock exchange. Thus, it is often made up of independent directors.

While there is some diversity in the way the audit committee functions internationally, the directors that serve on the audit committee oversee the financial reporting process, selection of the independent auditor, and receipt of audit results. They typically assist the board with governance and oversee financial reporting, internal control, and the risk a management system.

The audit committee normally works with many inside and outside experts. It is often empowered to hire outside resources and expertise to perform their responsibilities.

Primary Purpose

The primary purpose of the audit committee is to review and recommend approval by the full board of the financial reports prepared by management. To do so, they hold regularly scheduled meetings and maintain a connection between the board, the financial management of the company, internal auditors, and independent auditors.

While the audit committee has various responsibilities and powers, it is not the duty of the audit committee to plan or generate financial statements. This is the responsibility of the management team and independent auditors.

Role of the Audit Committee

All U.S. publicly traded companies must maintain a qualified audit committee to be listed on a stock exchange. The necessity of the audit committee can fluctuate from country to country depending on the law.

There are many responsibilities of the audit committee, including the following:

- Supervising financial reports
- Monitoring the choice of accounting policies
- Discussing risk management policies
- Overseeing the performance of the internal audit committee
- Supervising ethics (e.g., review of whistleblower calls)
- Monitoring the internal control process
- Hiring and overseeing external auditors

These responsibilities of the audit committee are assigned by a committee charter. Among other things, NYSE and Nasdaq Stock Market require that each company appoint at least three directors, all of whom must be independent, to an audit committee.

Essential Qualifications

At a minimum, each member of the audit committee must be financially literate. Accounting or financial management experience is important, if not required. One member of the committee must be a designated "audit committee financial expert," as required by the U.S. Securities and Exchange Commission (SEC). The audit committee members and the chairperson of the audit committee typically must be nominated and elected by the board itself.

What Is a Nomination and Governance ("nom/gov") Committee? Who Is Qualified to Serve?

This nomination and governance committee is a subset of the full board directors that has the power and responsibility to ensure that the board of directors is properly aligned to effectively address the strategic challenges of the company. The chair of the committee leads the process and reports results of decisions and recommendations to the full board.

It is the duty of the committee to have a succession plan for the board that ensures that the skills and characteristics of prospective directors have been properly evaluated and investigated. For a public company, it recommends to the board the proposed candidate(s) for nomination for election to the board at the next annual meeting of the shareholders.

It may also review and recommend changes to the full board of corporate governance policies and determine whether the board complies with its governance policies.

You are expected to not disclose the nomination committee's discussions or decisions outside the board. You need to be comfortable with being even more discreet than other directors.

You must understand how to clearly interpret issues that relate to the board, company governance, and the company's long-term strategic vision. You must know what is expected of every director at different times and what each director brings to the table. Such judgments must not only be unbiased but must also reflect the aims and objectives of the company.

The *Board Profile and Competency Matrix* worksheet in Appendix B can help you to identify the experience, knowledge, and skills that you can leverage for board service.

You will be trusted to carry out duties with utmost integrity. This means that members of the committee are expected to sustain the values of the company through a high level of integrity that will reflect whenever they are carrying out their duties. For instance, potential nominees of the committee are expected to be given purely objective considerations that take the company's strategic long-term goals and vision into account.

You must possess diverse experiences and sound knowledge about various fields. This will help you clearly and accurately evaluate candidates from various fields and backgrounds.

What Is the Compensation Committee? Who Is Qualified to Serve?

The committee, a subset of the full board independent members, oversees the compensation packages for the CEO and management. Some committees also focus on management development and succession planning.

In a public company, the responsibilities of the committee have increased significantly with the "Say on Pay" mandated votes by shareholders as required by reform legislation in 2010.

With increasing complexity of executive compensation and competition for the key talent needed by the company, you will need significant training and study of regulations and market conditions, so that you can have an excellent understanding of how compensation plans impact the company's goals and culture. The use of professional compensation consultants assigned to assist the committee is widely accepted. Having a member who has experience in human resources is becoming more common.

What Is the Role of the Board Chair? Who Is Qualified to Be a Board Chair?

The board chair is often seen as the spokesperson for the board and the company.

The articles of incorporation often provide for the election of a chair of the board. They may permit the directors to appoint one of their own numbers as chair and to determine the period for which the chair holds office. In many companies, CEOs also serve as chair; in other companies the role is separated.

The chair manages the board's business and acts as its facilitator and guide. This can include the following:

- Clarifying board and management responsibilities
- Planning board and board committee meetings
- Managing board composition and organization
- Developing the effectiveness and credibility of the board

Every board meeting must have a chair. He or she ensures that the meeting is conducted in an orderly manner, is properly attended, that all those entitled to may express their views, and that the decisions adequately reflect the views of the meeting. The chair often decides the agenda and might sign off the minutes on his or her own authority.

Typically, if no chair is elected, or the elected chair is not present within 5 minutes of the time fixed for the meeting or is unwilling to preside, those directors in attendance will usually elect one of their members as the chair of the meeting.

Often there is no special procedure for resignation. As for removal, articles of incorporation may permit the board to remove the chair from office at any time.

What Is the Role of the Lead Director? Who Is Qualified to Be a Lead Director?

Until recently, many firms combined the CEO and board chair position in one person. Today there is increasing discussion of the benefits of splitting these into two people. After Sarbanes–Oxley was passed in 2002, the SEC requires listed companies with nonindependent chairs to have a lead director.

A lead director is an independent board member who is usually elected by the independent directors. The lead director works with the board chair to ensure that the board carries out its responsibilities and is increasingly undertaking a wide variety of tasks.

How Does a Board Stay Effective?

A great board is always very diverse in perspectives, background, thought, and representation. After all, the board of directors must make important decisions for the company to assure its long-term prosperity. For example, the board may fire or hire a CEO or other members of the executive staff. And the board is ultimately accountable to the shareholders of the company.

While good governance is necessary for a functioning board, these practices can also help boards be more effective in balancing its numerous, and sometimes competing, priorities and goals:

- **Regular attendance at corporate board meetings**
  Attending regular board meetings is the hallmark of an attentive and responsible director. *All* directors must prioritize regularly attending meetings. Studies have demonstrated that regular attendance can truly impact the success of a company and its directors. Attending board meetings is a way to make important decisions; bond with other members; and share experience, knowledge, skills, and strategies. Board attendance records of each director must be reported to the SEC for public company boards.

- **Diversity of skills and experiences**
  To run a board successfully, each director must bring strategic and valuable experiences, insights, knowledge, and expertise. Their complementary skills and attributes can benefit the company and may even increase the company's revenue. It is important to have well-qualified, skilled, and collaborative directors.

- **Diversity of thought**
  On average, diverse directors make better decisions than homogeneous corporate directors. In addition to diversity of skills and experiences, it is a good idea to make sure that a board of directors also exhibits diversity in other categories such as gender, age, race, sexual orientation, national origin, and thought as they bring different perspectives of customers and stakeholders into the discussions.

- **Maintaining a clear and distinct role**
  One of the biggest wellsprings of contention may arise when the directors endeavor to overstep their roles from oversight to management. Directors are occasionally unclear about their roles. It is critical for the board to discuss important issues and oversee problems without managing.

- **Moral ownership**

  The directors are the moral owners of the company. It is important that they are people of high integrity with long records of flawless judgment. This way, their actions and words can inspire a company and its leadership to stay on course.

- **Implementing key policies**

  Among the greatest difficulties for organizations is having a clearly articulated mission and purpose. Companies can frequently lose all sense of direction in hectic administrations. Generating a clear idea of where the company is endeavoring to go or whether it has been successful should be the primary focus of boards.

- **Well-planned board of directors and committee meetings**

  It is critical for a successful board to have a general meeting plan that spans the entire year, with a set agenda before each meeting. This way, the directors will plan, meet regularly to discuss issues in a timely manner, and make sure that their meetings are productive.

- **Self-improvement responsibility**

  Each director is responsible for his or her own competency. Therefore, it should regularly inquire about the skills and experiences each director is bringing, the gaps that need to be filled, and the time frame for filling any gaps.

CHAPTER 2

Types of Boards

Many people who refer to corporate boards of directors think only of large public companies. As noted earlier, there are many other types of boards, such as startup boards, various types of private boards, family-owned boards, advisory boards, and nonprofit boards. Serving on these non-Fortune 500 boards can be a valuable professional and personal experience. It can also serve as a launching point to leverage into a position on a public company's board.

This chapter further describes various types of boards and the opportunities that they present. Educating yourself about *all* the choices in board services will assure success in obtaining both the director position and satisfaction of board services. After all, we generally make better choices after we are educated. Board service is no exception!

What Are the Different Types of Boards?

All types of boards need strong leadership and operational powers regardless of purpose and size. Every board needs a complete delineation of expectations and responsibilities. They must also present a clear framework to support the organization to the best of their capabilities, including interacting with stakeholders and other company leadership. Their job is to do the best things for the organization, even beyond the walls of the board room.

As you know, boards are important because they are responsible for effectively serving their companies. There are generally four types of boards. Each has its own unique responsibilities, major roles, and compositions. Here are the four types of boards:

- **Nonprofit boards**
  Nonprofit boards serve a tax-exempt organization. Directors on these boards make a commitment to a cause that that they are

passionate about. Board service for nonprofits often involves volunteering, fundraising, or philanthropic donation.

The primary reason to serve on a nonprofit board should be an interest in the nonprofit's mission and impact. Serving on a nonprofit board is a satisfying experience when your interests are aligned with the mission of the nonprofit organization.

Depending on who else is serving, how structured and organized the board is, and what your specific role is, nonprofit board service may be an opportunity to learn and network while working hard for a cause that you believe in. Depending on the nonprofit, prior board experience may not be required. One benefit is that you can learn fiduciary responsibility by serving on a nonprofit board.

These opportunities are almost never paid but can be well worth it in terms of fulfillment and experience. Consider being clear about your responsibilities, time commitment, and expectations to make sure there are no surprises. Also, consider attending a few meetings to determine whether you really connect with the board's mission, structure, and people.

To be clear, serving on nonprofit boards may or may not help to obtain a position on the for-profit board. Almost always, service on the nonprofit board does not lead to an appointment on the for-profit board. While this should not be a primary reason to join a nonprofit board, depending on how the board is structured, who serves, and the level of notoriety of the nonprofit, serving on a nonprofit board may be a useful learning or networking opportunity. Connections that you make with corporate board members or chief executive officers (CEOs) on a nonprofit board may be a great way to get recommendations or referrals to a for-profit board. If a corporate board member sees the value that you can bring to a nonprofit board and your overall approach to board work, he or she may be the perfect recommendation for your next step in board service.

- **Advisory boards (aka councils)**
  Advisory boards offer fine expertise and excellence to other boards or executives such as the CEO. They often complement other

functional areas of the organization, such as the management team or task forces.

For a startup venture, the advisory boards are often highly prioritized. Founders often set up an advisory board as part of the initial planning stage. Over time and as the startup matures or transforms, other advisory directors may be added. A well-managed and well-structured advisory board can enhance any startup and organization, whether be it profit or nonprofit.

Advisory boards are non-governing boards with no fiduciary duties. Because of this, some do not agree that advisory boards should be called "boards." Even if you prefer to call them "councils" instead of boards, they still merit consideration. Advisory boards often offer valuable professional opportunities and are a great way to start your board journey. Plus, those boards may be the precursor to a fiduciary board at a company. If the CEO sees you as an asset here, he or she may lobby for you as a true board member when such a time comes. And other advisory board members may recommend you for other boards if you shine in this role.

Advisory boards may provide a good first introduction to corporate board service. If you join one, consider being clear about your expectations and what you will be able to contribute.

- **Private company boards**

The working zone of the private company board is vast. Private company boards serve not only small businesses but also companies of all sizes. Some private companies are quite large. These opportunities include large multinational private companies, co-ops, venture-backed startups, family businesses, and numerous others.

Private company board service opportunities exist in many industries and geographies. It is worth exploring the richness and wealth of your options when it comes to private corporate boards. Private boards do not have as many legal and regulatory requirements as do public corporate boards. Therefore, private boards are often great starting blocks for corporate board service.

Many directors also find private boards more satisfying and less structured than the board service on public company boards.

Your private company board experiences will widely vary across companies, industries, and geographies.

- **Public company boards**

  Public company boards are highly regulated. As a result, they are very structured. It is a serious, time-consuming role, though it may be well-compensated. As a public company director, you must allocate significant time to prepare and attend meetings, serve on committees, and fulfill other responsibilities, especially during times of crisis. Public corporate board positions take significant time to obtain as they are relatively rare and very selective and exclusive.

What Is a Startup? What Is a Startup Board?

A startup, usually a privately held business, is a new business that is still being built. For new entrepreneurs, starting their own company is a huge undertaking. Most of them think that a startup board is not of importance, at least for the groundbreaking process. Over time, many startups that survive the first few years may rethink this position as they educate themselves about their industry, their business, and the value that directors bring.

The Need for a Startup Board

For every company, a board may be very important, if not necessary. When an entrepreneur is building her empire, she will assess her business, its needs, and the value that she hopes the prospective director would bring. The truth may be that startup businesses can be successful with or without a startup board. However, often the need for a board arises if there is an investor who demands that a board be formed. A board may also become necessary if an entrepreneur wants to address certain needs of her company.

Startup Board Composition

The people an entrepreneur chooses for her board are critical to her business' performance. As time progresses, she may need to involve more people with certain expertise, knowledge, or experience. Executives, senior management, officers, former regulators, and industry leaders are among the people who may be included on a startup's board. They may become key decision makers and even be involved hands-on in a startup (aka a working board).

The Role of the Startup Board

Because there may not be a lot of information available about a startup, completing your due diligence on a startup company and its founder is especially important. Every startup board or advisory director should work well together and have a shared understanding of the company, its founders, its goals, its investors, and its numerous other stakeholders.

What Is the Difference between a Board of Directors and an Advisory Board?

A board of directors, also known as the governing body of the institution, company, or organization, is a group of individuals that are normally elected to act as representatives of the stockholders to establish corporate management-related policies and to make decisions on major company issues. The board of directors' key purpose is to ensure the company's prosperity by collectively directing the company's affairs, while meeting the appropriate interests of its shareholders and stakeholders.

Normally, under the law, only governing directors and officers hold fiduciary responsibility to the institution, company, or organization where they serve. Fiduciary responsibility entails three duties to the institution, company, or organization where they serve. These are commonly known as the fiduciary duties of care, loyalty, and obedience. The corporate board of directors may be present in both for-profit and nonprofit organizations.

In contrast, an advisory board comprises of a few individuals whose work is to provide advice to the CEO, other executives, senior managers, or the board of the company to ensure the effective functioning of the company. Usually these are appointed not elected roles. Most importantly, the members of the advisory boards do not owe a fiduciary duty to the institution, company, or organization where they serve.

In addition to these key distinctions between a board of directors and an advisory board, the following may also apply:

- **Terms, conditions, structure, and code of conduct**
  A board of directors follows very strict terms, is elected at a certain regularity, has fiduciary obligations to shareholders, must abide by strict laws and regulations (e.g., Securities and Exchange Commission (SEC), New York Stock Exchange, Nasdaq Stock Market), and follows a prescribed strict code of conduct.

  In contrast, advisory board opportunities tend to be more flexible, informal, less regulated; require fewer terms; and almost never impose fiduciary obligations to shareholders.

- **Responsibilities and working**
  A board of directors generally advises across disciplines, subject matters, geographies, and problems. They tend to focus on all material issues that may affect the long-term returns for company's shareholders.

  In contrast, the members of the advisory boards tend to be much more specialized on a certain subject matter or problem. In fact, they are often engaged because of their expertise, experience, or achievement. Therefore, its involvement tends to be much more limited in scope and duration.

- **Influence, power, and voting rights**
  There is a major difference in the voting powers of a board of directors and an advisory board.

The members of a board of directors are the governing body in their company. They have a superior position in the company, with ample powers resting with them. A board of directors has the legal right to create or alter certain decisions and directions of the institution, company, or organization.

Advisory boards are less influential and powerful. They advise the CEOs, leaders, senior managers, or the board of directors on certain subjects. They do not have to take the advice from advisory board members. It is normally completely voluntary to follow an advisory board's advice. In other words, if the advisory board's advice is not followed, there is nothing an advisory board can do in terms of enforcement.

How to Join a Startup Board of Directors or Advisory Board?

Any intentional board search starts with self-reflection. Ask yourself if you are ready to join the board, how much time you can invest in board service, and what you expect from the company that you are going to join. You will need to determine what your specific target audience is as well as a process to leverage your network.

It is also very important to honestly consider the following issues:

- **Understand the time commitment**

  To join a startup board and to serve it successfully you need hands-on experience and a well-built network. Securing these is, of course, a time-consuming matter. If you are on one of the board's special committees, you must also dedicate time to solving any unique problems that arise. Before joining a board, be clear about the time that you can give to your job and your organization to make it successful. In the context of a startup it is even more important to be clear about the expectations and time commitment because much of the information is usually private and the needs of the company may be rapidly shifting as it is being built.

- **Clearly articulate your value proposition to the board**

  You will have a huge responsibility as a startup director. The board will expect several commitments from you that may include financial investments, philosophical boundaries, and much more. Only you can articulate what you can offer, and only you can understand your true capacity. Ask yourself: Considering your education, experience, and expertise, what value could I bring to the companies I would like to serve? Also, make sure you know the unique angle that you want to bring to the board, such as a fresh industry perspective or a perfected, expert financial strategy. Am I able to give to this startup what it expects to gain from our relationship?

- **Craft your target market**

  Determine your target market and know everything about it. Research will uncover the essentials, such as location, size, and industry. What companies am I a particularly good fit for? What industries? What experience, knowledge, and expertise do I have that is particularly valuable to them, and why is it so valuable? Make sure to ask the startup founders and senior personnel about the skills, expertise, and experience they are looking for to fill.

- **Actively conduct due diligence on the company that you want to join**

  After knowing your own strong points, do the reverse by conducting due diligence on the startup. What follows is a list of basic items to research before you decide to join a startup:

  ○ Check all the signed reports that are prepared generally for the governing body or the team of directors of the company.

  ○ Read all the signed resolutions of the committee, including written copies of notices and all the paperwork details of the shareholders, partners, and the members of the company.

  ○ Review all the press releases and news that are issued by the organization or are relevant to the organization.

  ○ Inspect a complete summary of the personal relationships; business relationships; and affiliation details of the company's customers, shareholders, members; and so on.

  ○ Know more about the business structure and strategies of the company, including areas where the business needs to expand or where you can use your knowledge and skills.

  ○ Research the skills, capabilities, and reputations of the founders, investors, and current officers and directors.

What Is a Startup Advisory Board? What Are the Factors to Be Considered before Joining a Startup Advisory Board?

Many startups also create an advisory board. An advisory board offers advice to the board, CEO, or to another executive that runs the startup. An advisory board offers business insights, expertise, industry knowledge, or experience. An advisory board also assists with other important business transaction decisions. Consider the factors below in assessing startup advisory board opportunities.

- **Familiarize yourself with existing directors and advisors**
  What directors and advisors are already included in the startup? Do you know them? If not, you need to learn more about them and their roles. You may eventually have to create a rapport with them. Make sure you know the professionals you will be working with and what they do. This will help you work more effectively and efficiently.
- **Identify with the company's values**
  Understand the company, its history, and values. What are its goals, mission, and plan? Does its niche interest you? What value will it add to your personal or professional life? This will be a key determinant in deciding whether to join a startup advisory board.
- **Determine compensation**
  Advisory directors may be paid in one way or another, and it is important to understand what that means. For the first few years of the company's life, expect payment through equity of the company only, though there may be notable exceptions.

  If you were expecting cash, then your reasoning may not be in line with the startup's objectives. If this is a problem for you, you should be prepared to have a conversation about it, likely with the CEO and cofounders. Depending on your involvement with the startup and its industry, it is not unusual for a startup advisory board to award up to 1 percent in equity, depending on your background, involvement, and commitment.
- **Consider possible challenges**
  Every company has its challenges, including startups. But this does not mean that you should not join a startup advisory board. It means that you should carefully educate yourself about the advisory board opportunity that you are considering. One person's challenge is another's valuable learning opportunity.

When you have an advisory board offer on the table, it is a good idea to do your research and think it through to ensure your fit considering your experience, expertise, availability, and relationship with other directors. Consider reaching out to other advisors to gain insights about the role, industry, and compensation.

What Is a Family Business? What Kind of Board Opportunities Do Family Businesses Have?

A family business, another example of a privately held business, is owned by an individual or family, often consisting of two or more generations. The ownership lies in the family and the generations to come. Achieving success within a family business may become challenging as the family and its wealth increase. Navigating the conflict among generations may be particularly challenging.

There are several board opportunities that a family business can provide. Board opportunities at a family business are based on four different kinds of governance models. They include compliance boards, insider boards, inner circle boards, and the independent (sometimes called "non-influential") boards.

- **Compliance boards.** Compliance boards are meant to comply with the laws and regulations that the family business must meet. The family can decide to appoint someone, either a family member or someone outside the family, to serve on the company's compliance board.
- **Insider boards.** On the insider boards, it is all about the family—no outsiders allowed. Each family member is given a position, and each one is responsible for ensuring he or she plays their part for the success of the family business. The leadership of an insider board will change with different family generations.
- **Inner circle.** The inner circle board is partly family and partly friends. It is often a one-person affair where the company's CEO selects people who are trustworthy within their individual inner circle. All three of these board structures are associated with and influence the company's chair of the board in one way or another.
- **Independent boards.** To get rid of that influence, a family business can choose to take a different direction. The independent board is made up of outside directors that have no association with the CEO. They are indifferent to personal matters, and they work professionally. These directors bring their own insights to the company's board, and each one expects that their opinions will be

regarded. As a result, transactions are more corporate, and business deals are made solely to make the entity prosper. The independent board has immense benefits on a family business, precisely because the directors have no direct ties to the company.

What Can Independent Directors Bring to a Family Business?

Independent directors can do a lot to add value to a family business board. In fact, hiring directors that have no relationship to the business or the family has incredible advantages. Comparing the board of a family company to that of a public company, the family business boards tend to be more flexible. This is because they are usually free of U.S. SEC regulations and stock exchange listings rules that must be adhered to by public companies.

Once a family business embraces an independent board of directors, they may include them in many, if not all, company matters. This may lead to a very hands-on board experience that some former or retired executives crave. Thus, as an independent director, there are numerous ways you can add value to a family business.

- **Operations and risk management**
  Every business—including a family business—needs a board that has operations experience. As a director, you may provide necessary data and benefits to help the company's executives run a smoother operation.

  This also relates to risk management. All companies, public or a family business, are prone to risks. As an independent director you may be well positioned to flag, address, and mitigate various risks. The independent directors are uniquely positioned to offer solutions and techniques to control risks.
- **Significant skills and assessment**
  A board may provide the missing skills to facilitate the company's success. Family businesses may not create a diversified board, especially because inner circle boards are made up of family members and friends. This can be a problem because diverse boards are

important for business success. However, by creating an independent board, a family business can attract directors with diverse skills, knowledge, expertise, and experience to improve the performance of the company.

- **CEO evaluation and succession debates**

  CEOs are not always hands-on, or they may not have the right knowledge, experience, or expertise. Under such circumstances, independent directors may add value. As a director, you may have knowledge, expertise and experience on the different business aspects that the company can benefit from, in which case you can advise the CEO.

  Similarly, sometimes the next person in line for family business succession is not the best choice. They may have little knowledge the business, not be interested, or need orientation prior to being appointed as the new company president. Independent directors can help the outgoing CEO choose and prepare the best successor for the business.

- **Contributing to corporate strategy**

  Developing the corporate strategy for a family business lies in the hands of the company's leadership and managers, most of whom may be family members and friends. However, before implementation, the board needs to discuss and approve strategies. This is where the independent board of directors may add a lot of value.

  For every goal that a family business wants to achieve, members of the board of directors may significantly contribute to what is right for the company and create strategies to do so. Due to their diverse experiences, they may also be knowledgeable about more effective ways to achieve different goals. Without an independent board, family businesses may face the issue of different agendas, which can result in a poor choice of strategies.

- **Important investments and transformational transactions**

  As an independent director, you may be well positioned to differentiate between valuable and bad transactions and investments. Based on your experience, expertise, knowledge, and connections you may advise the CEO and family business leaders to enter better transactions and make more sound investments.

- **Monitoring company performance**

  Once the corporate strategy is applied to the company's perform-ance, there needs to be a follow-up and monitoring. This is also where an independent director may add value by inquiring about the progress.

- **Influencing company behavior to the community**

  The success of a family business is also dependent on its behavior in the community. The services they offer may be part of the larger com-munity where they live and hire their employees. Therefore, it is only right to give back and be involved in the community. As an independ-ent director, you may be in a good position to build community rela-tionships, serve as an ambassador, and generally help the company to grow a positive reputation in its immediate community and beyond.

- **Managing external communications**

  Finally, you may be well positioned to help with external com-munications. Shareholders, investors, family members, industry insiders, regulators, and authorities are all part of the bigger pic-ture, and maintaining a great line of communication with them is paramount. This is where the guidance from an outside director may be very valuable.

What Are Advisory Boards?

An advisory board is a group of people who give non-binding, strategic advice to the boards of a company or organization, CEOs, or other exec-utives. The nature of the advisory board is informal and flexible.

Although an advisory board has no role to interfere in cooperative mat-ters, they may serve as great recognition of one's skills and provide opportun-ities to network. Occasionally, serving on an advisory board can be a stepping stone toward larger roles including leadership roles and board service.

Examples of Advisory Boards

There is a lot of variation in how and why advisory boards are created and operated. Therefore, you need to do a lot of due diligence and understand all your potential commitments and obligations before you join.

While there may be others, what follows is a list of examples of advisory boards that are somewhat common. Ultimately, it is up to a company to decide what advisory board to form, if any, and how to run it.

- **Risk advisory board**

  The role of the risk advisory board may vary from company to company, depending on the scope of the business. The main role of the risk advisory board is often to bring people together for risk management. The risk advisory board can also help the board, the company leadership, and numerous other company stakeholders in making difficult and strategic decisions.

- **Environmental advisory board (EAB)**

  The EAB tackles social and environmental responsibility. The EAB reviews the new strategies that other boards are planning to ensure that the company's actions do not harm the environment. In some companies, they also advise boards or executives to come up with sustainable products and use products which are eco-friendly.

- **Innovation advisory board**

  This is a new way to address any product and innovation made by the company. The innovation advisory board helps the company create new innovations which are more beneficial to the company. Often the goal is to help the company to lead innovation or keep up with changes in technology. This board may also help to improve the design of new innovations and get them trending in the market. This advisory board helps to sustain the company's competitive position in the market.

- **Technology advisory board**

  The technology advisory board helps to upgrade the technology of the respective company. A technology advisory board often recruits young, talented members, who may not be hired as regular employees due to their very high salary expectations or because they are still in school or have other commitments. This role involves an understanding of social media, data analytics, and mobility, which are the main topics of today's technology advisory boards.

Why Consider Serving on the Advisory Boards?

Advisory boards may have a lot to offer to some professionals. The advisory board team has a wealth of expertise that can help you to enhance your decision-making skills and develop your network. Serving on an advisory board can also provide an opportunity to work on cutting-edge problems, at a reputable company, or on high-profile projects. What follows are examples of five ways an advisory board can create value for professionals:

- **Intellectual challenge**
  Advisory boards provide you with social, creative, and intellectual capital. The members focus on specific issues and may be valuable advocates for a company or organization.
- **Learning to manage risks**
  Advisory boards play an important role in risk mitigation. Due to their knowledge, experience, expertise, and connections they may provide a valuable experience to mitigate risks.
- **Staying ahead**
  Advisory boards are usually composed of subject-matter experts and industry leaders. Therefore, they may be helpful for a professional to stay current and relevant.
- **Anticipating the next big thing**
  Similarly, to stay ahead, serving as an advisory board member may help professionals to anticipate the next big thing, especially as part of the technology advisory board. After all, technology is transforming all industries around us, and every professional is doing their best to keep up.
- **Expanding and deepening your networks**
  Members of advisory boards can help secure opportunities in other industries and geographies. They may prove to be a valuable source of information, resources, and referrals in the future.

CHAPTER 3

Why Serve on a Board?

Being asked to serve on a board may seem like the ultimate compliment. It shows a certain level of achievement and recognition that your skills are valued outside of your own organization. Directors also meet interesting people, expand their network, and grapple with stimulating issues. Independent public company directors are also often well paid.

Yet board service may not be for everyone. It takes a lot of time to both secure a board position and serve. It is important to answer the question: Why do *you* want to serve on a board?

There is no shame in ultimately deciding to postpone or not pursue board service. This chapter focuses on the reasons to serve on a board. It also covers the risks of board service as well as important questions to self-evaluate whether board service is right for you.

Board opportunities may be powerful. They may add value to your resume, boost your experience, provide opportunities to grow, allow you to work on challenging problems, let you set corporate strategy, help you raise a public profile, provide opportunities to influence others, empower you to make important decisions, and many more.

There are several reasons why more and more professionals are considering board of director opportunities. The benefits of serving on a board of directors can hardly be ignored by anyone who is aspiring to take their career to the next level. Some of these benefits include the following:

- **Intellectual challenge**
  Intellectual stimulation is the primary motivation for many professionals who choose to join a corporate board. Strategic planning, navigating mergers and acquisitions, planning for chief executive officer (CEO) succession, and many other milestone events are

learning-rich opportunities, regardless of whether you have been involved with them before.

- **Gain more expertise and experience**

  As a director you may learn to handle complex issues from different point of view and under different circumstances. You will also gain more industry experience and obtain a wider perspective.

- **Grow your network**

  In addition to new knowledge, experience, and expertise, your network will likely grow substantially. You will get a chance to build a network with fellow directors, investors, partners, industry thought leaders, CEOs, competitors, vendors, and many others.

- **Develop your career**

  Serving on a board will also give you an opportunity to be in a strategy role without being consumed by daily execution realities and challenges. This will provide you with more time to develop your career from a different, more strategic angle.

- **Additional income stream**

  Serving as a director, especially at a large public or private company, may offer substantial compensation. Although there is a lot of variance in compensation depending on experience, industry, company size, and many other factors, total compensation often has both cash and equity components and may be substantial. If involved in a startup, you could see incredible compensation if successful, or serve for several years for zero reward.

- **Be a leader**

  Serving on a board may increase your leadership abilities. In fact, you may find that other opportunities come to you because of serving as a director. For example, you may get other board opportunities, interesting job and consulting offers, and opportunities to speak. You can also be an industry thought leader and enjoy an increased public profile.

- **Understand board governance**

  Serving on a board will most certainly increase your corporate governance knowledge and help you to become more fluent in navigating the boardroom, C suite, and various other important relationships. Just like most things in life, comfortably navigating a boardroom comes with time and experience.

There are, of course, numerous other benefits of board service. Ultimately, corporate board service is a gratifying experience that many professionals find rewarding and lucrative. It is worth considering, preparing for, and obtaining!

How to Prepare for Board Service?

When filling a director position, most companies look for someone who has a lot to offer in terms of leadership qualities and experiences. Yet serving on a board itself also provides an opportunity for professionals to further develop leadership skills and take them to the next level.

The board needs performance, not just promises. Directors need an open mind, curiosity, and integrity. They need problem-solving and crisis management skills, as well as the ability to readily adjust with changing circumstances. They also need motivation, especially newer members, to bring out the best in others.

Therefore, it is very important for a director to realize that leadership opportunities are not all about running the company. Leadership in the boardroom is also about setting a direction for executives and senior managers who in turn can guide employees.

To grow as a leader and be well positioned for board opportunities, it is helpful to develop the following key skills as soon as possible:

- **Get used to regular involvement**
  Boards are looking for someone who is regularly involved, has had hands-on operational experiences, and is committed to attending every meeting in person. In fact, regular meeting attendance is considered a mark of excellence by most directors and required by the U.S. Securities and Exchange Commission.
- **Build board skills**
  Understand what a board does, how their role differs from executives, and how to create efficient consensus among senior professionals from different backgrounds. These and many other skills should be developed throughout one's career.
- **Build a wide and deep network**
  Many directors bring the value of having a substantial network. Therefore, it is worth developing your network throughout your

career. Once you get on your first board position, continue building your network further to help your company and create other
board opportunities for yourself. In fact, one of the best rewards
of joining a board is having better networking opportunities.
These increased networking opportunities allow you to get connected with people who will contribute positively toward your
development.

- **Proactively build your reputation**

  Prospective directors who have spent a lifetime of building a positive and strong professional reputation in certain industries are an
  asset to any board. Make sure that you proactively build your reputation and credibility over time. People will begin to see you as an
  expert and authority in your field of discipline, which will bring
  you new opportunities.

- **Strengthen your skills, experiences, and expertise**

  Of course, substantive skills, experiences, and expertise are valuable to companies looking for prospective directors. It is important
  to build these qualities throughout your career. This enables you to
  become an expert and provides you with opportunities for growth,
  including board service.

Cultural Awareness on a Board: What Is It, Why Is It Important, and How to Leverage It?

As globalization has become the new normal, the corporate world has
also seen an increase in cross-border recruitment, transactions, sales,
exchanges, partnerships, and much more. Many companies are intentionally looking for directors who can represent global opinions and
problem-solve in the increasingly competitive corporate world.

Many academics and business analysts have given their own defin-
itions of "cultural awareness." Fundamentally, cultural awareness is the
foundation of communication. It involves the ability to standing back
from ourselves and become aware of our cultural values, beliefs, and perceptions. It may include one's ability to recognize cultural, behavioral,
historical, and philosophical differences.

Depending on the company you are considering, cultural awareness may be an important skill for serving on the board. It is important to hone this skill throughout your professional life.

What Skills to Develop

- Have knowledge and self-awareness not only about your own cultural background but also other cultures around the world.
- Be open to the thoughts and beliefs of others and practice a non-biased approach when tackling various business issues.
- Be open to communication where the flow of ideas is not restricted and barricaded by cultural differences. Communication is the key to cultural awareness.
- Be adaptive to all kinds of situations, including those that are unfamiliar.

How to Leverage Cultural Awareness Skills to Get on a Board

- **Be social**
  Socialize with the team. In some cultures, ensuring that everyone gets to know each other well before they start to work together is prioritized. When a new member is introduced to an organization, there is often a welcome party, which is the best time socialize and get to know each other before beginning serious work.
- **Know about local business practices and how they may differ from others**
  Every culture has its own set of values. It is important to know them and practice them. This shows that you are not only here to do business but that you are adapting to the work tradition. Examples can include practices related to business cards, greetings, and meals.
- **Settle on common grounds**
  It is not possible for everyone to have the same approach to all business practices. No two countries have the same working conditions. At times, you will have to understand the economic

background and tactics of other parties to effectively tackle issues. It is important to have a repertoire that allows you to emphasize common ground rather than being rigid and firm on issues.

What Are the Major Questions to Ask before Joining a Board?

To assess your board readiness, consider asking yourself a series of questions before you begin your board journey. What follows are some questions that will help you self-assess your board readiness.

- **Why do I want to become a director?**
  What compelled you to want to serve on boards generally and this company or organization specifically? What is the reason that you are a good fit here? Try to narrow down why you want to serve for this specific organization. Why do you want to associate your reputation with it? What value will you bring to the company or organization? For the relationship to be sustainable, the beliefs and values of the company and organization must echo your own, and the association must be mutually beneficial.

- **How passionate am I about this organization or company?**
  A quality organization needs and deserves passionate directors who genuinely contribute to the company's objectives and inner workings. A board is not for those who simply take up space. Ask yourself how passionate you are about the organization's vision, mission, and objectives. Never take a director position just to look good or add some perceived value to your portfolio. If your heart and your mind are not in it, it will not be beneficial. Serving on a board is a big commitment and time investment that you should take seriously.

- **Am I aligned with the company's vision, mission statement, and core values?**
  The privilege of serving on the board is to raise your voice to make a positive difference. Your role as a director is to guide the company and its leadership to stay on track and thrive. You can only do so when you are aligned with the company's mission statement, vision, and core values. Ensure that you have an in-depth

understanding each of these facets. Gather valuable input from all levels of the company, including other directors and the leadership.

- **Do I understand and embrace the organization's history?**

  Once you serve on a company's board, it is now your business. You need to understand what the company has gone through in the past as well as the current landscape and direction. Research recent staff changes, and compare forecasts to reality. Audit statement history, projections, timelines, previous performances, public records, and word-of-mouth news are all important things to know about. The company's past may be the looking glass into its present and future, so take advantage of it.

- **Are there any negative issues with the company? If so, have I concluded that I can be effective? Are we really a good fit? Is this a good board for me?**

  Insist on honesty and transparency from the start. You can never serve a company optimally if some points are left unchecked or in the shadows. Ask tough questions and make sure you get intelligent and timely responses. Create an expectation that you will ask and address the tough questions. This is the time and place to be transparent and act with integrity. Finally, select board opportunities where you will have the opportunity to prove your value and where your skills and personality are a good match. Do not pick a board because it seems "prestigious." Very few things are more disappointing in board service than a poor fit between the director and a company, the director and the existing board, or the director and the management.

- **Do I respect the CEO, the management, and the board?**

  If you do not have respect for this leadership team going into a board role, it is unwise to take this board seat. The only exception might be that the board already knows that it is replacing the CEO and you will have the opportunity to determine the new leader.

What Are the Risks That Come with Serving on a Board?

Before joining a board, it may be a good idea to pause and consider how you can mitigate any potential risks. What follows are some questions you should ask yourself to assess the risk profile of a board service opportunity and your risk tolerance. It is worth considering these questions both before you join a corporate board of directors and periodically after you join.

- **Does the company have comprehensive** directors and officers liability insurance (**D&O**) **coverage? Does the indemnification agreement protect you?**
  Every company needs comprehensive directors and D&O. Ask what the insurance policy covers and to what extent. It may also be a good idea to work with a professional to get you comfortable with the policy and the indemnification agreement.
- **What are the risks of joining the company or organization?**
  If the stock price sinks, the directors can be sued—this is normal and completely expected. In fact, public company directors should be comfortable with this reality. It is the responsibility of the board to maintain financial strategies, and manage sales and marketing plans. Directors can be questioned about the process of their decision making at any time. Therefore, a director should understand corporate governance, perform their duties diligently, engage in a good decision-making process, continually educate themselves about the risks of their business, and work closely with legal and other professionals.
- **Will joining the company increase my reputational risk? If so, to what extent? Should I still join? If so, how will I mitigate these risks?**
  Bad board actions or decisions may affect the reputations of its directors, even if you were not involved in the decision or it predates you. If you are part of the board, people may have reasons to question your credibility and judgment.

  Your insurance will not cover reputational risk if you are serving on a board. And the damage to your reputation can be very costly and often irreversible. For example, it may affect your ability to serve on other boards. Only your due diligence may reduce the chances of your reputational risk.

  Reputational risk is not at all new for companies. However, in today's digital age, news of the risks spreads faster than ever, reaches everywhere, and can be impossible to delete or contain. The reputational damage that a director suffers may be severe and long-lasting.

Therefore, it is important to understand and learn as much as you can about the company—where it has been, where it is, and where it is going—before you join as a director. Consider learning as much as you can about the company's current board, its executives, its founders, its investors, other stakeholders, and its history.

- **Is there a criminal risk associated with joining the company?** The chances of criminal risks are very rare for the board of directors, especially in the United States. You will find this kind of rare incidents only in the most egregious fraud cases. Of course, your due diligence about the company and its stakeholders may help you identify the main criminal-risk red flags. After you join the board, consider staying alert and keep your eyes open. Evaluating risks is what good directors do regularly.

- **Is there a financial risk associated with joining a board?** The financial risk of serving on a board in the United States is low, if you follow established corporate governance rules along with any company-specific rules. Thus, understanding the company's charter, bylaws, other corporate documents, and corporate governance is important.

  It is also important to understand how you are compensated. For example, what percentage of your compensation may be in equity that you are expected to not sell while still serving as a director? Are there explicit restrictions on what you can sell and when?

- **Is there a cross-border risk associated with joining a board?** In the United States, this risk is also generally low. Moreover, D&O should cover cross-border risks. Of course, you may want to look more closely at the enforceability and the language of the policy.

CHAPTER 4

How to Get Board-Ready?

A large part of your board journey requires getting board-ready. You will likely spend just as much time strategizing and improving yourself as a candidate and identifying your target as you spend pursuing and interviewing for specific positions.

This chapter outlines the process of getting board-ready, from developing key skills to identifying board positions. Specifically, it will discuss what to consider before deciding to serve on a board, how to choose the right board, how to position yourself to better your chances of being asked to serve on a board, specific steps to take throughout your career to become board-ready, what characteristics, attributes, and skills to develop, and how to start building important relationships early.

What to Consider before Deciding to Serve on a Board?

Historically, board service has been a part-time commitment for retired executives. However, this is changing. Boards are increasingly becoming open-minded about who they consider. Some boards are also rethinking their expectations from their directors.

To join a board, you need to be sure that your skills, experience, knowledge, and expectations are aligned with the company's expectations and requirements. Moreover, before finalizing your corporate board position you must know the board position in depth, and what it means to be a successful director. The questions below are useful to consider as you contemplate your board journey.

- **What and how valuable is your knowledge, expertise, experience, and time?**
  How valuable is your time and expertise for various boards? Where do you add the most value? How valuable is your knowledge,

experience, network, and dedication? Which of these personal aspects may be attractive and to whom? How to identify your value proposition is further discussed in the next chapter.

Use these factors to crystallize the value you bring to a board. Why is this characteristic valuable to a company? How valuable is it? Be very selective with how you use your time and expertise.

- **What kind of company can you benefit with your knowledge, expertise, experience, and time?**
  Once you identify the unique value that you can bring to a board (further discussed in the next chapter), it is useful to zero in on what kind of company would most benefit from your value proposition. Maybe you are well trained and knowledgeable about the textile and fashion industries, with a decade of operational experience in consumer athletic wear. If so, be prepared to research, identify, network, and approach companies and their stakeholders who may benefit from this value. If you are an experienced IT specialist for both the legal industry and business-to-business data companies, then you must figure out what kinds of businesses as well as which specific businesses will find your insights valuable.
- **Why do you want to serve on a board of directors?**
  As with any undertaking, it is worth understanding your motivations and requirements. What follows is a list of questions that you should consider asking yourself.
- Why do I want to serve on a board?
- What motivates and inspires me?
- What industries am I passionate about?
- What new skills do I want to learn?
- Do I want to hone my existing skills?
- How will I make a difference?
- How will this decision benefit my career or life goals?
- What is my lifestyle, and how does corporate board service fit into it?

To decide whether you want to serve on a board, consider clearly understanding and articulating the value you bring to a board, who can benefit from it, and why you want to serve. You can focus on how to join a board only after you define your goals, your value proposition, and organization that is right for you.

What Is a "Right" or "Good" Board?

It is important to determine the right boards for you. Otherwise, you may be wasting your valuable talent and time aimlessly applying and networking. Consider the steps below:

Inventory and Understand Your Skill Set

To select the right boards, you must first inventory and understand your skills. What is your knowledge, education, expertise, experience, and skills? Take time to reflect on your accomplishments, achievements, work history, education, businesses, and other milestones to make sure your list is complete. Then you can spend time identifying your most relevant board-related skills and matrix those that best communicate your value.

Figure Out Who May Want Your Skill Set

Spend time matching your skills, with both general industries and specific companies and individuals. Is your knowledge, education, expertise, experience, and skills a better match for private boards, advisory boards, nonprofits, or public company boards? Once you have an idea of where your skills match up, you can start considering the right board for you.

Articulate Your Skill Set

By joining a board of directors, you must be able to add value to the company. The process of identifying and articulating the value you bring may take time. Here are some examples of what you may bring to the board:

- Technology and risk mitigation for a consumer electronics company
- Nurturing new talent and managing talent across the globe
- Finance and operation experience for food manufacturing companies
- Sales or marketing experience and expertise for software as a service companies
- Global commerce, export, and import experience for gas and petroleum companies

In What Industries Do You Want to Focus?

If you have transferable skills you can also consider serving on a board in a different industry to prove your skills across industries.

It is important to consider all industries where your experience, expertise, and network may be relevant. For example, if you have cybersecurity expertise, do not just think of your industry or the security industry, as virtually most large companies regardless of the industry are currently focused on protection of their data. Change your mindset and become versatile for corporate board positions.

Diversify Your Interests

Be more specific about what you are looking for in terms of the type of company, responsibilities, compensation, and board experience. In the end, there is no objectively perfect board position, just as there are no objectively perfect directors. Nonetheless, there are directors who are perfect for specific board opportunities. By being specific about what exactly you are looking for, you may realize that the best opportunity for you is one that you have not considered before.

Appendix A provides an *Identify Your Target Board Opportunity* worksheet, which can be used to identify the right board-service opportunities for you.

Generally, What Are the Steps to Become a Director?

Becoming a director is a matter of strategy, time, research, and patience, with skill and culture matching to a company and their board. To fulfill your goal to become a director, at a high level, you must follow these steps:

- **Define and articulate your board profile and elevator pitch**
  You need to be able to articulate the value that you will bring to a board in a written board profile and elevator pitch that you deliver verbally. Because your board profile and elevator pitch are relatively short, you must be very selective in what you include and exclude. Some people start with a board resume/CV and board biography and then reduce them to a few sentences that capture

their value proposition. I recommend starting with a clear written board profile and then use your board biography and resume/CV to expand it and add more color. Nancy Sheppard, who contributed and edited this book, recommends starting with the resume/CV, then board biography, and then narrow down to the pitch by highlighting first the three to five key accomplishments that are board-worthy. Of course, once you have your board elevator pitch, practice delivering it! Delivering your board elevator pitch out loud can help you to deliver it more confidently and identify any changes that you need to make to perfect it over time.

Appendix D features many sample board profiles that you can use to start drafting your own board profile.

- **Create your board resume/CV and board biography**
Based on your profile develop your board biography and board resume/CV. These documents showcase your value by highlighting the skills, experience, and knowledge that you will bring to the board. In sum, these documents communicate the same information, just with a different level of details and slightly different format.

Appendix E features many sample board biographies. Use these as an inspiration.

- **Network intentionally**
Many board opportunities come through word of mouth and referrals. They are rarely advertised! Networking is extremely important to becoming a director. Start networking as soon as you identify the value you bring to a board, and target companies and industries where what you bring would be of great value.

It is prudent to aim to meet directors, chief executive officers (CEOs), chairpersons, and other professionals related to boards such as attorneys, accountants, consultants, cybersecurity experts, and numerous others. Do not be afraid to be bold and share your goal of joining a board. Be clear about what type of board you want to join and what your skills are! Remember most people are not mind readers!

Of course, you should be professional and diplomatic when you deliver your elevator pitch, which will summarize the value that you would bring to a board. Assure them about your value, skills, expertise, and experience. Ask them what they have seen on various boards and about the needs of those boards. Then ask them what they can do to help you serve on a corporate board or if they can introduce you to those who already serve on or work with corporate boards.

It is important to be clear and specific. Ask to be introduced to the companies that you think match with your value. Also ask them to introduce you to CEOs, chairpersons, board members, and other relevant board-connected professionals at your target companies.

- **Select a mentor and advocate**

  Seek out a trusted person from your network, preferably one who serves on or is connected to a board. This person may share their ideas, advice, experiences, introductions, and knowledge. Sometimes this person may be at your current job, such as the CEO of your company. Others, however, may find it easier to have a mentor outside of their current organization.

- **Consider joining a nonprofit board or advisory board**

  Consider serving on nonprofit board or advisory board that you are passionate about before pursuing a corporate board position. This can help you gain hands-on experience, showcase your talents and expertise, learn corporate governance, determine whether you enjoy board service, and network. It can be a (relatively) low-commitment way to test-drive being a director. Of course, make sure that you are truly passionate about the organization you are joining. That is a must for any board position! However, joining a nonprofit board does not make you corporate board-ready, unless you have the skills and leadership experiences needed. It can be a great place to network with board influencers who then may recommend you to a for-profit board because they see how you "show up" in a board environment.

What to Do Now to Become Board-Ready?

Serving on a corporate board is a challenging journey for everyone. You will need lots of patience and planning to start. Take the time to be strategic. Serving on a board can be a huge challenge with great responsibilities. Even extremely talented, qualified, and experienced professionals often struggle to secure a board position, especially the first one.

Some Steps That You Can Take Now to Reach Your Board Dream Sooner

- Give your 100 percent to your "day job" and always do your best. In the end, you want to be the best business and profit and loss (P&L) operator that you can be, and have your skills and accomplishments recognized. P&L is covered more in depth later in this chapter. To make yourself board-ready, you need to achieve some significant success measures in your career. So the very best way to get a board position is to focus on accomplishing and succeeding in your own career.
- Relevant operational and leadership experience related to the value that you would bring to a board is necessary to serve on a corporate board of directors. Seek out opportunities to gain this experience in your current position.
- Being an expert in your industry may improve your visibility and reputation, which may be helpful in your board search.
- Start small to achieve something big. Consider starting with a non-profit or advisory board to gain experience, expertise, exposure, and connections.
- Be clear about your motivation, values, skills as well as your reasons for serving on a corporate board.
- Become known as a thought leader by writing and speaking on a few key topics that are important to the success of a company.
- Develop and keep an external networking and visibility focus. Make the time even if you have a very busy job. Too many people keep their heads down with internal duties for too long in their careers.
- Use opportunities to be involved in board activities and board meetings at your company.
- Keep in touch with professionals in your target industries, especially those who are considered experts and those who serve on boards. Most board positions are filled through a network.

- Do your research and understand governance responsibilities by reading, doing webinars, and educational programs. A director has considerable obligations and responsibilities. Make sure you understand how the boardroom works, what the law requires of directors, and where directors can get timely advice.

Questions You Should Be Able to Answer If You Are Ready to Serve on a Corporate Board

- How much experience do you have as a senior executive leader in any private, public, or nonprofit sector? A minimum of 10 to 15 years is a good place to start.
- Are you ready to work a minimum of 200 to 300 hours every year as a director, in addition to your existing obligations?
- Will you get the support of your current company's senior executives or directors for your new role and time commitment needed?
- Are there company policies that will prohibit you from serving on a corporate board of directors?
- At a minimum, are you comfortable and experienced in understanding and navigating a boardroom?
- Do you have your professional governance designation or certification (Chartered Director (C.Dir) or Institute of Corporate Directors, Director (ICD.D)) from a corporate director organization, institute, or college? These are more essential if you seek a public company board.
- Do you have any nonprofit or for-profit board-service experience in a director, observer, or board presenter or assistant capacity?
- Can you work as part of a team by understanding the board's dynamics and by creating and following good governance?
- What do you know about the liability, responsibilities, and functions of a director? Do you understand the risks of serving on a board of directors? Are you familiar with ways to mitigate these risks?
- Do you have the capability to maintain separation between a management role and the role of a director? Will you be comfortable with determining high level strategy and letting the executives and senior managers run the company's daily business?

- Do you have the skills to at least proficiently understand and read financial statements regularly?
- Are you ready to take responsibility for the critical areas of a company? Can you solve these issues with your prior experience such as digital media, risk management, mergers and acquisitions (M&A), international markets, cybersecurity, and long data?

What Are the Characteristics and Attributes of an Ideal Director?

A successful and compelling director requires powerful, effective, and collaborative individuals. Here are some of the key attributes of good directors:

- **Passion**
  Directors should work for a cause, industry, or organization that they are passionate about. This way they will be truly connected with the general mission and enjoy their board service more.
- **Experience**
  Having the specific knowledge, experience, expertise, and skills that are valued by your target companies is the best way to be considered for board positions and enjoy your board service.
- **Time**
  Many professionals will consent to serve as a director without acknowledging the time commitment that it will require. Besides standard meetings, there may be additional requirements to assume the responsibility of other tasks. Therefore, it is important to be clear about expectations and time commitments.
- **Attentiveness**
  Directors must be proactive and not wait for issues to come to them. Board service requires individuals who can remain in front of the industry, their field, and their company's problems, rather than continually being in a responsive and passive state.
- **Toughness and collegiality**
  Directors must be prepared to go up against difficult and complex issues, and go the extra miles through clashes. At the same time,

they should be conscious and inspire cooperation. Being able to balance these skills and seemingly conflicting values is an art worth perfecting. Be open to healthy disagreements with others, but also be able to eventually accomplish resolutions and keep a working relationship and connection in place.

- **Highest level integrity, good judgment, and confidentiality**
A high level of integrity and a track record of good judgment are paramount for a corporate director. After all, the directors must make very important decisions, lead high-profile companies, instill investor confidence, and help companies through transitions and important milestone events. Many board decisions and discussions are confidential and may not be shared outside of the boardroom.

- **Strategic thinking**
Directors lead the company's strategy, which gives quantifiable objectives and goals for the company. The director role is very separated from the role of daily management. It is important that directors are comfortable and proficient with setting and keeping an eye on a strategy.

- **Preparation**
Effective directors get their work done. They go to meetings educated and prepared to examine concerns and issues. They take the time to review and understand all important documents to administer effective strategies and objectives.

- **Enthusiasm for learning and service**
The most effective directors are always ready to learn, cooperate, ask tough questions, and ultimately lead. They are driven and enthusiastic about serving others.

- **Knowledge**
Directors must understand the goal and mission of the company. They are acutely aware of where the company has been, where it is going, and how it will get there.

- **Eye for diversity**
A good board incorporates and includes individuals from different fields and backgrounds, with diverse experiences, expertise, and knowledge, to guarantee that the organization is well rounded in its qualities and strengths.

How to Develop Key Skills to Serve on a Board?

To join a board, you need to identify your unique skills, experiences, knowledge, and achievements. The goal is to become more adept at precisely defining your specific skills that is desirable. What follows are a few ways to get there.

- **Passion for a company, its mission, products, services, and industry**

  As a director, you must be passionate about your company and its mission, products, services, and industry. You must know all the important stakeholders and have good working relationships with them. Heavily research the company and get to know its key players and stakeholders. Aim to make deep connections so you can develop a true passion for all aspects of the company. This is required for all directors, whether be it for public or private companies. Passion creates a drive to succeed and overcome all obstacles.

- **Effective decision maker**

  Decision making is paramount for a director. A director must be comfortable educating herself about complex subject matters where she has little or no expertise, making decisions by bringing consensus, and coming to quick and accurate decisions in a crisis. Fumbling or getting confused is not an option. Working in different situations and organizations will provide you with a strong foundation to make decisions by consensus, and stay coolheaded, even in a complex situation where you are not an expert.

- **Innovative thought leadership**

  Boards set long-term strategy and are responsible for the long-term success of an organization. To this end, it is important to adjust to changes in the economy, foresee technological shifts, spot trends in your customers' tastes and preferences, and engage in out-of-the-box thinking in a strategic, calculated, and intentional way. Being open-minded and enriching directors with your innovative ideas is essential for serving a company.

- **Staying active in your field and industry**

  Action is part of your board service. While director positions tend to be part-time positions, it does not mean that they are part-time commitments. In fact, joining a board is a commitment to full-time, lifetime learning. Whatever the value you bring to the board, you must commit to further developing, refining, and upgrading these skills. Moreover, to set a long-term strategy for your company you will need to understand and be involved in your company's industry and know key industry stakeholders. In other words, joining a board involves a sizable commitment in and out of the boardroom.

- **Long-term strategic thinking**

  Directors provide the strategic long-term vision for the company, normally to maximize the returns for their shareholders (true for public companies). To this end, you may be making decisions that affect financial strategy, management strategy, technology strategy, innovation strategy, expansion strategy, and many other key decisions. Practice thinking in the long term and understanding how different areas of a company interact. This can involve research, networking, and expanding your current position's responsibilities.

- **Impeccable judgment, wisdom, and integrity**

  Boards are generally looking for people who not only have enough experience but are also known for their impeccable judgment, wisdom, and integrity. After all, the board sets long-term strategy for the company, leads all stakeholders, and inspires confidence in investors, government officials, and many other important players. Therefore, impeccable judgment, wisdom, and integrity are paramount. Ensure that your reputation in this regard is flawless. If you are still in the beginning of your career, keeping this in mind can be especially useful.

- **Diverse and relevant skills and expertise**

  Most decisions to fill a board are at least partially driven by skills that a board may need given where the company is and where it is going. Therefore, it is very important to understand and articulate what skills and expertise you have. Make sure that you develop a diverse array of skills to increase the chances that you are the "missing piece" a board is looking for. Also practice articulating your skills in flexible ways that show your value to a board. There is a difference between saying "I have legal experience" or "I am a lawyer," and "I am skilled at constructive risk analysis."

- **Interpersonal skills and collaborative personality**
  Communicating and establishing a relationship with the other directors is a vital skill for a director to be effective and efficient. This is especially important for relatively large boards because the decision-making process may already be slow and frustrating. Therefore, building coalitions, active listening, and choosing your battles wisely are crucial skills for any corporate board of directors.

How to Identify and Address the Missing Skills for Board Service?

Relevant skills are crucial for you to become a director. You need to be acutely aware of the skills and experience that you bring, as well as the skills and experiences that you do not have or have not fully developed. Here are some tips to identify and fill in missing skills:

- **Lead with you your core skills, experience, and knowledge**
  It is important to design your corporate board biography and resume in a way that highlights your core experience, expertise, and skills which are valuable at the board level. The aim is that you join the board based on your core competencies and that the bulk of the interview process is spent in those areas. Practice discussing your skills, experience, and knowledge in measurable and specific ways to make a compelling case that you are the ideal director for the company that you are targeting.
- **Research and identify the skills, experience, and knowledge of the similarly situated current directors**
  Consider what skills, experiences, and knowledge the current similarly situated directors bring to the company that you are either targeting or are like the one that you are targeting. What critical skills, experiences, and knowledge are you missing? Can you fill these missing attributes?

  Focus on highlighting the skills, experience, and knowledge that are missing yet necessary that you can gain from being in the current target board.

  To answer all these questions, you will need to do extensive research. For example, besides researching your target company and its specific needs and stakeholders, consider also researching the skills that the corporate board looks for when appointing a new director. Look for trends for director recruiting in similarly situated companies and see how you can help your target company.

- **Fill your experience gap**

    You will have to be honest with yourself and identify the skills that you are missing. If you are still a few years away from applying for your first board position, consider taking strategic assignments or job positions to develop these skills. If you are already pursuing board positions, ask yourself whether you can get up to speed through education, reading, research, or interviewing colleagues that may have the skill that you are looking for. Also, consider highlighting the value and skills, experience, and knowledge that you have instead of what you are missing.

- **Highlight your unique skills, experience, and knowledge that are valued across industries, geographies, and companies**

    Certain skills, experience, and knowledge are universally sought after across industries, geographies, and companies by all types of boards. Some examples are experience entering new markets, managing financials, targeting new demographics, leading through difficulties and transitions, expertise in understanding and dealing with regulators, taking a company public, structuring M&A, facilitating post-merger integrations, leading global expansion, orchestrating a digital transformation, launching emerging and disruptive technologies, managing risks, having foreign language skills, and changing company culture. Consider emphasizing on these skills and experiences on your board resume and board biography.

What Factors Are Considered in the Selection of Directors?

The following categories of factors are considered when prospective directors are evaluated:

- Experiential attributes, such as education qualifications, accomplishments, industry experience, expertise, and knowledge, as well as functional experience.

- Demographic attributes, which include generation, gender, geography, ethnicity, and diversity of thought.
- Personal attributes, which include personality, interests, values, propensity to collaborate, judgment, integrity, and cultural adaptability.

While other attributes may be considered as well, these categories of factors often create a baseline that permits companies to more deliberately shape their boards. These factors are often addressed during the candidate evaluation process, either implicitly or explicitly, through interviews, meetings, references, psychometric examinations, and other evaluation techniques.

Why Should Directors Master P&L and Financials? How to Leverage Your Financial Experience?

P&L stands for "Profit and Loss," which refers to a comprehensive financial statement that is prepared at the end of a period to display the costs, revenue, and expenses of a company over that period. It is more like a financial summary which shows whether a company has been able to make profit or loss over a given period. When the income is more than the expenses, profit has been made during that period, and vice versa.

Why Should Directors Master the Company's P&L and Financials?

- **Better decision making**
  Directors are involved in setting the strategy of the company, which means that your decisions are very important and will impact the bottom line of the company. Knowledge of P&L and financial statements will help you to make more well-informed decisions. Finance is a corporate language, and directors are expected to be at least proficient if not fluent. In fact, financial literacy is so critical that it is virtually impossible to get on a board without this skill. If you are not a finance professional, consider cultivating this skill throughout your career.
- **Analysis of revenue earning departments**
  Mastering the figures usually presented in a P&L and other financial statements enables a director to properly analyze the company's

performance. This allows a director to have a deeper understanding of what is going on in the company. All financial statements tell a story. The question is whether the prospective directors can read it.

- **Projection of revenue**
  Directors must know how to set targets. P&L and other financials are vital when projecting revenue and planning. In other words, they are critical to strategic leadership.

How You Can Leverage P&L and Financial Experience

Understanding and being proficient in your company's P&L and other financial statements is crucial to your success as a director. Therefore, financial literacy is a plus for any corporate director candidate, even for those that bring other different talents to the company. Consider educating yourself about P&L and other financial statements in your current role. Take assignments where you are responsible for a large budget and must make projections. Also consider volunteering for other opportunities that will increase your financial literacy. This can make you a more attractive candidate for board service.

If, however, you are a former chief financial officer, controller, or some other finance professional, consider prominently highlighting this skill in a clear and a measurable way. All boards have finance professionals, and their expertise is highly valued and sought after.

Are Board-Placement Services Useful?

The recent hype about board service, especially for women and diverse candidates, is real. It seems like everyone is getting on board—or at least trying to. The increased interest in board service has led to a proliferation of board-placement and board-readiness services. These services offer appealing packages, intended to help prospective directors become desirable candidates and find the positions of their dreams. Many seem like the "magic ticket" to a professional's first board position.

Professionals ask many questions about these services. Are they useful? How much do they cost? How should a hopeful board candidate choose from the many options? As much as I like to advise and encourage potential board candidates, it is difficult to answer these questions. They are just too subjective! Choosing a board-placement or board-readiness service is like choosing a car: The right one depends on who you are, your goals, and your preferences. It is not an easy process, but by asking the right questions, you can get a feel for whether a specific placement or readiness service is right for you.

Not sure where to start? Here is a list of questions to ask any board-placement or board-readiness service:

- **Geographic concerns**
  Where are the services offered? Where are the candidates placed? Does the service offer board-placement or readiness services locally, nationally, and internationally? At a minimum, you want to make sure that the board-placement or board-readiness service meets at least some of your geographic needs and aspirations.
- **Industry and network fit**
  Does the service offer boards from organizations in a wide variety of interest areas to address your goals? Does the service have connections in your industry? Does it place people in public, private, startup, or nonprofit boards that you are interested in? Does it have connections and trusted relationships with the executives, decision makers, and influencers? It is important to ensure that the service's expertise, core competency, and network are of use to you.
- **Track record of success**
  Does the service track its success metrics? How often does it place candidates? How frequently do the candidates that it places work long term? Do its candidates tend to stay on boards where they are placed for at least 3 years? Does it publish its rates online? If not, why? Does the service provide a relatively comprehensive list of companies that it has helped? How long has the service been in existence?
- **Process logistics**
  If a service considers itself a board-matching service, how many board positions does it offer each month or year? How many organizations does it serve regularly? Does it let you interview with more than one board opening at a time? It is also important to

understand what, exactly, you are signing up for. How exactly does the algorithm or process work? How involved is the service, beyond simply identifying candidates? Is there someone at the service who will be personally familiar with and knowledgeable about the company, their needs, and their experiences and then match you with the right board opportunity? Or will you be invited to a board fair, or provided with a list or search engine to pursue board opportunities on your own? How does the service ensure quality control for matches? Finally, what are the credentials of the individuals who will be performing your search?

- **Promises made**

  What promises are made regarding your success? Does a firm do a "reverse search" agreement in which you pay a fee to be connected to boards? If so, is a board seat guaranteed? Do they introduce you to board members? Board-matching firms that are successful typically charge large fees.

- **Money matters**

  Who will pay for placing you, how much, and when? Will the company pay? Are you expected to pay? Is the payment tied to reaching any milestones? Are there different packages for different candidates or companies?

- **Included and additional services**

  Does a board-readiness service provide assistance, such as writing your board biography? Does it provide you coaching regarding your network and your presentation skills? Does it provide constructing an elevator pitch and interview coaching? Does it share research about the company, its executives, and its directors? Does it provide a matching service, and if so will the service stay involved throughout the matching process to answer questions and keep the interview process on track? What other value besides helping you present yourself as board-ready and qualified does the service provide?

- **Good to know**

  You may also want to understand whether the board services specialize in certain demographics such as hiring initiatives for women, placing diverse candidates, or locating first-time board candidates. You may also need to know whether the service will allow you to work with other board-placement or board-readiness services simultaneously.

This list may seem overwhelming, but because board service is such an important career step, every question is important. After all, you would not purchase a car without making sure all your bases were covered. Similarly, when choosing the right vehicle for this exciting career move, you need to shop smart and stay proactive to separate out the lemons.

Appendix C provides a list of *Board Search Resources*, which includes some board-placement services.

CHAPTER 5

Director Roadmap: Practical Steps to Become a Director

The board journey is an intentional process. You must be prepared to articulate your unique value proposition, forward essential board documents such as board biography and board resume, and build relationships intentionally and strategically.

Here are some tips that I consistently hear from seasoned directors to get both the first and the subsequent board appointments:

- Work with your employer's support to secure your first board position.
- Patience and persistence are critical to finding your first board opportunity.
- Understand what types of boards you target and what trends affect your industry and target companies.
- Intentionally brand yourself in ways consistent with your value proposition, in all channels and communications.
- Always protect your reputation.
- Understand your value and be clear where your expertise fits best.
- Never stop networking.
- Always be prepared and shine.
- Take visible leadership positions inside and outside of your companies.
- Tell everyone that you want to serve on a board.
- Develop a board campaign strategy to reach decision makers and influencers, and stick to it.
- Stay informed about board trends and your industry.

- Protect your integrity at all costs.
- LinkedIn is your friend. Communicate your brand there clearly and consistently.
- Write and speak on issues related to boards and your unique value proposition.
- Channel executive presence, gravitas, and confidence.
- Build genuine and authentic relationships intentionally.

This chapter will guide you through articulating your unique value proposition, elevating your profile using LinkedIn, crafting your board documents such as your board biography and board resume/CV, and intentional relationship building and networking.

What Is a General Roadmap for Becoming a Director?

To create your corporate director brand, you will need your corporate board profile and elevator pitch, board biography, and board resume/CV. You must also intentionally and authentically build and nurture important relationships. This section generally describes what each component entails.

Each component has a unique flow, style, and tone. Each could stand alone and interact with others. Combined they make a powerful presentation of you, your skills, and your expertise. Specific content, data points, credentials, accomplishments, and achievements must be highlighted to make a compelling case of what makes you a strong prospective director.

Be very clear about your target audience in terms of industry, size, geography, and other relevant factors. Is it large cap, mid cap, or small cap company? Do you target companies in certain life cycles or industries? Are they in services, medical devices, technology, financial, or something else? Do you target certain companies? Are they private, public, private equity (PE)-backed, startup, family business, or something else? Focus your components to your clearly identified targets to increase your likelihood of success.

These components are much more than what you have done or tasks that you have completed. You need to emphasize your experience and results at the highest level of organization. Do not focus on tactics, tasks, or responsibilities. Actively connect the dots for the reader to make a case of why they need you as their director.

All these components communicate what you bring to the board in different ways, in different contexts, and in different circumstances. Understanding what these components are, how they are used, the sequence of events, how these components can be combined, and how they may interact will help you focus correctly and use proper tone at each stage.

Stay away from jargon, puffery, or self-promotion for all these components. They should not be part of your journey because they will undermine your reputation and you will come across as an incompetent rookie.

Use your judgment and consider circumstances and timing in deciding what written documents to use. There are no clear rules as to when to use various board documents. For example, board biographies are generally good to inspire interest. You could send your board biography to someone whom you briefly met at a conference and who liked your elevator pitch. It is effective to send your board resume/CV when a certain level of interest is shown. For example, it is appropriate to send a board resume/CV after the board biography has been forwarded and the recipient wants to learn more about you.

Finally, make sure that all your written components (and their multiple versions if you have customized them for more than one target) are well written, revised, and edited multiple times. They must be complete, up to date, and readily available. These documents will likely have a relatively long life span and will be circulated to numerous important people who make critical decisions. For example, you will use them as you network, facilitate introductions, meet search firms, connect to board decision makers and influencers, get feedback on your candidacy or qualifications, and in numerous other ways.

Finally, invest time into doing this work and building these components. Often you only have one opportunity to put your best foot forward, and give a first and likely a long-lasting impression of yourself as a prospective director. Make sure you do not waste any opportunities, and leave a good impression every time!

There is no absolute format that is agreed upon by everyone, but this outline of board documents is well accepted by many board experts. Formats should be clean, easy to read, and as concise as possible, as most are quickly reviewed by board members, board influencers, and recruiters.

Feedback from board members can be helpful to make sure you have high-lighted yourself in a manner that typically resonates with those who are looking for board members. A caution, however, is that many different people would view board biographies and board resumes/CVs, so be aware that there is no perfect way to draft these documents that all viewers will like.

- **Board profile (aka unique value proposition or elevator pitch)**
  Your board profile is a concise statement of up to three to five sentences that clearly articulates your unique value. A board profile should be a concise summary of your overall achievements, operational experience, noteworthy companies, and why these skills and experience provide board value.

  Appendix D features many sample board profiles for your reference to start drafting your own board profile.

- **Board biography**
  A board biography is a one-page narrative that expands your board profile and further details your professional and board experience and accomplishments with metrics that validate these accomplishments. The one-page limit is considered a rule by many. If you cannot concisely express your experiences and value, then some may wonder if you would be able to be concise in the boardroom (which is seen as a must by most directors and CEOs). Its goal is to provide a few more details in articulating the unique value you bring to the board and to inspire the reader to be further intrigued to learn even more and ask for your board resume/CV.

  Appendix E features many sample board biographies. Use these as an inspiration. Appendix F features a template that you can use to start drafting your own board biography.

- **Board resume/CV**
  Your board resume/CV is fact-based inventory that complements and expands on your board profile and board biography. It can begin with a short summary of your overall accomplishments and includes all relevant achievements, skills, expertise, experience, and knowledge in chronological order and bullet form.

  Appendix E features many sample board resumes/CVs for your reference to start drafting your own board resume.

Intentionally Build Relationships

You must actively network to become a director. Here is the general process of networking for a corporate board of directors:

- Identify your target audience to set your plan and policies for networking.
- Identify professionals who you want to work with and build positive professional and authentic relationships with them.
- Create a plan and system to consistently interact and be helpful to professionals with whom you want to build positive professional and authentic relationships.

What Is a Unique Value Proposition (aka Board Profile or Elevator Pitch) and How to Articulate It?

In your board profile, be sure to communicate a clear vision and have a target audience in mind. Who do you have in mind? What kinds of boards do you want to serve on? What do you have to offer to a board? How are you different from other candidates? What is your achievements record and in what kinds of companies, industries, and circumstances? What events and outcomes have shaped you?

Even more importantly, you need to answer the following questions to articulate your unique value proposition: Why would a board find you valuable? What do you bring to a board that other people do not? What is your superpower?

Make sure your board profile is direct and well written, using complete sentences. Emphasize your skills, expertise, experience, qualifications, knowledge, and achievements. Also emphasize important roles that you have filled, such as leadership roles or any role where you have made an impact. Highlight your skills such as collaboration and consensus skills. Consider mentioning your involvement with well-recognized, iconic Fortune 500 and Standard & Poor's 500 companies.

Avoid using jargon and use leadership wording. Write short, carefully crafted, three-to-five-sentence paragraphs. The goal is simple—to inspire the reader to be intrigued, to be enticed to learn more, and to ask for your board biography.

Your unique value proposition should contain both your "wheelhouse" expertise and major career accomplishments related to this expertise which will also be relevant, appropriate, and valuable for your target board.

In crafting your unique value proposition statement (aka elevator pitch) the following are good practices:

- Highlight your unique skills, background, experience, expertise, and education. Stand out and be uniquely valuable.
- Be clear about the industries and companies that you target.
- What in your background will they find appealing and valuable?
- Experiment with different value proposition statements to find the one that works best for the board that you are targeting.
- Emphasize your skills, expertise, and experience. They are more transferable and relevant than you may realize.

Your unique value proposition should be a statement that you eventually internalize and can deliver verbally or in writing effortlessly, naturally, and in a way that compels other professionals to want to learn more about you.

Your value proposition focuses on concretely answering what value you bring to a board that other people do not. Your value proposition will provide useful information for you target board decision makers and influencers.

Also, consider narrowing down your expertise to your wheelhouse or superpowers and verify these with data, metrics, and other compelling indicators that back them up.

The following are some questions to ask yourselves as you experiment with a few different value proposition statements. Do some due diligence to crystalize your board profile and cultivate your corporate authentic director brand. It is well worth it to think about these questions and answer them over time. Practicing self-reflection and clarity will help in perfecting all your board papers, not just the board pitch:

- What are your best skills, expertise, experience, and knowledge? Be specific about your experience and focus it toward board services. Describe examples that illustrate it.

- Who can you influence?
- What value do you bring?
- What credentials do you have?
- What are your contributions and achievements? Describe results in a measurable way such as profits and loss (P&L), patents filed, and other metrics.
- What milestones have you reached for companies? Was it innovation, reorganization, transitions, expanding, mergers and acquisitions (M&A), initial public offering, restructure, growth?
- What did you manage? Was it people, products, P&L, government relationships, board, equipment, foreign entities, or something else?
- What are your key traits that others value? Are you ethical, collaborative, diligent, or defined by some other qualities?
- What are you an expert in? In what area do other professionals seek your advice?
- What are your senior management experiences?
- What has been your track record?
- What are the trends in your professional history? Why were you hired for various roles? What results did you achieve?
- How did your job transform? How did you keep up with new roles? How did it change you in the process?
- What pressures and difficult forces have you been able to address? A security breach, sudden departure of an executive, change in brand strategy, weather disaster, political instability, regulatory instability, major risks, publicized litigation, or an unexpected investigation? What did you learn in the process?
- What are your leadership qualities? Focus on your leadership progression to come across more subtle and less self-promotional.

Here are some examples of unique value proposition for two professionals:

Jill is a financial service and fintech executive and advisor who leads strategic transformation in the face of rapid technology, regulatory, and market changes. She brings a blend of consulting and corporate executive experience for industry leaders including Bain, PayForward, and MasterCard. She utilizes 25 years of experience repositioning and scaling companies through innovation, new product, market, talent, capability development, and M&A. She is well positioned to add value in the boardroom of a company in the payment processing space.

Here is another one:

Nancy is a C-level executive and advisor with expertise in mobile, consumer products, and connectivity that form the backbone of today's IoT. Her strengths in developing strategy, and launching and running fast-growth, innovative e-commerce businesses has grown from her leadership in scaling two consumer online businesses to $500M during her 20 years with Company A and Company B. Her experience on the boards of a startup private company acquired by Company C adds to her overall knowledge of bringing significant value to founders and investors.

Appendix D features many sample board profiles that you can use to start drafting your own board profile.

How to Use LinkedIn to Become a Director?

LinkedIn is the most established way to raise your board-ready profile. In fact, no director journey is complete unless your LinkedIn profile articulates your unique value proposition. LinkedIn is an effective tool to gain visibility with your target company and its directors, the chairperson, the CEO, executives, and other stakeholders.

It is important to have the right LinkedIn profile—one that is an extension of your board pitch—that highlights your unique value proposition, reinforces your professional brand, and boosts your opportunities, visibility, and overall presence. Today, an effective LinkedIn profile is certainly a powerful and necessary board-brand building block for all prospective directors. Be sure that your LinkedIn profile is consistent with all your other board papers. It must encompass and expand on what you have in your board profile. Moreover, it cannot contradict your board profile, board biography, or board resume. Today, LinkedIn is the most powerful tool that I know for anyone who wants to activate her board brand.

Moreover, building up your network on LinkedIn is important because many board searches either start on LinkedIn or progress to LinkedIn profiles after the initial interest stage. It would be a significant mistake to ignore LinkedIn.

Keep in mind that LinkedIn's page design resembles a resume. LinkedIn is not optimized for senior leaders or prospective board candidates. So your profile may not be appropriate. Consider to intentionally shape the perception of your LinkedIn profile through tone, framing, and inclusion and exclusion of facts strategically.

Here are the ways to optimize your LinkedIn profile:

- **Be clear about your audience**
  There may be conflict between your current employment and board audience. Identify and decide your target audience and optimize your LinkedIn profile. This will shape the impression and perception through tone, content, repetition, pictures, media, words of others, and curation to make sure that your target audience experiences, interprets, and appreciates you. Your LinkedIn profile is not a confessional—do not list everything. Strategically and selectively choose only relevant information that complements your board profile, board biography, and board resume.
- **Highlight your skills**
  Establish as consistent, unified, and stable image that will give others a framework from which to understand you, your experience, and what you bring to the table. Your skills can be highlighted in numerous ways on LinkedIn: skills endorsement, postings, blogs, profile pictures, videos and other media, job descriptions, utilizing the introduction section, and other ways. Showcase board-appropriate skills. For example, focus on leadership, not management. What are you leading? Is it a division, company, initiative, multibillion-dollar project, or something else? Also, focus on strategy and result, not in the weeds, details, or tactics. Are you leading innovation, global expansion, new markets, or something else? Stay consistent, selective, and clear about who you are in all your LinkedIn activities.

- **Actively and intentionally broadcast on LinkedIn**

  LinkedIn allows you to change and modify your profile as much as you want. For example, you can add work experience or certifications and then broadcast these additions to your LinkedIn connections. If you take on an exciting speaking opportunity or start working with a nonprofit, make sure to update your LinkedIn profile and share the change with your network. This will give you an opportunity to shape your professional reputation and develop audiences around certain subject matters.

- **Add relevant keywords to your profile**

  Identify and add relevant keywords to your LinkedIn profile so that board recruiters and others can easily find you in a sea of other candidates. Give yourself some time to choose the right keywords first and then build your profile around them. This way you will stand out because you will more consistently show up in relevant searches.

- **Update your profile photo**

  Upload a professionally taken profile photo on LinkedIn. It is the first thing that people see in your profile, and you want to make a good first impression. Make sure that your picture is polished and projects the presence of a dignified director. Avoid casual or low-quality pictures. Also consider adding other media—pictures, videos, press releases, and other links—throughout your profile to add interest to your page.

- **Improve your introduction and headline**

  Update your LinkedIn introduction and headline to get more attention from recruiters and others involved in finding and evaluating prospective directors. Your headline is located right beneath your profile name. Use important keywords there to optimize the search results. Be sure to use the word "director" or "board member" to signal your interest or experience in boards. In fact, it is useful to think of your headline as a very distilled elevator pitch! Find an original slogan, tagline, or a phrase that represents your unique value proposition.

- **Board-appropriate recommendations**

  Leverage recommendations on LinkedIn intentionally. Be sure that the recommendations emphasize your board-appropriate skills, expertise, qualities, experiences, and background.

- **Other sections to update**
  Make sure your contact information, at least an e-mail, are included for your connections to see. Update your certifications, honors, projects, and awards with relevant information. Do you have a video of a keynote address you gave? Consider imbedding it in your LinkedIn profile if it is relevant.

- **Be social and stay regularly active on LinkedIn**
  Do not be shy! Self-promotion may seem unnatural, but it is important to embrace social media and being active on social media does not have to come across as self-promotion. Also, consider joining relevant groups on LinkedIn to gain insights and credibility. These could offer a fruitful way to connect and stand out as a subject matter expert. Being social on LinkedIn will increase your brand presence and help you build board equity.

  Stay socially active on LinkedIn to gain and maintain visibility. Here are some examples of how you can become active:

  Generally, boards are looking for a confident, respected, and presentable prospective director. They are looking for leaders with good judgment and high integrity. If you want to become a director, you need a distinct, positive, visible, and memorable public profile on LinkedIn.

  LinkedIn is a good start for all professionals! If you can only stay active on one platform, engaging and staying active on LinkedIn is the correct choice for most professionals. Depending on your industry and how social you would like to be, consider joining other social media platforms such as Twitter. The goal is to amplify your unique value consistently with your corporate board resume and biography.

Why Is a Board Biography Important? How to Write It?

Whereas a board profile is a short paragraph of your expertise, experience, impact, qualifications and qualities, a board biography is of one page that further elaborates details and complements your board profile.

In general, a board biography is a reflection on the leadership roles a professional has held throughout her career. It should not be confused with a board resume/CV. A corporate board biography aims to express the professional's unique value, skills, expertise, experience, and knowledge. The format is more narrative than a rigidly formatted, facts-based board resume/CV with bullet points.

Use your profile as the framework ground when you create a board biography. The details in the board biography must complement, echo, and expand on your board profile. Include details such as your work experience, especially any board experience, relevant achievements, and notable accomplishments.

It has a brief introduction and then it highlights skills, major deals, experiences as a director, and matrices that further highlight your unique value proposition and board profile.

Identify the gaps in the information in your short profile and build on them to tell a more compelling and colorful story. To do this, intentionally choose additional information and facts about you to build a compelling board biography.

For example, one way to do this is to paint a unique progression and perspective at a high level and emphasize your vision and strategy. For example, did you go from an entrepreneur to an advisor? What different perspectives do you bring? Carefully package the facts to guide your readers. Moreover, consider emphasizing a track record of success and impact on enterprise or division that changed a business in a positive way.

Nancy Sheppard, who has worked with women on their path to the boardroom since 2014, provides these tips on creating a memorable and effective board biography.

General Tips to Craft an Effective Board Biography

- Understand your audience and what matters to them.
- If you are not following board issues and trends, then you need to start, so that you can understand what is on their minds. The more you appreciate what is on the minds of directors at your target companies—size, structure, and so on—the more you can tailor your board biography to the specific needs that boards are addressing.

For example, a large public company is much more likely to be more interested in Environmental, social and governance issues than a Series B company that is focused on rapid growth.

- Your board biography will evolve. As your targets for industries, companies, and boards become more specific, what you emphasize adapts and evolves over time.

- Embrace what you have accomplished. While you do not want to sound conceited or have a big ego you must tell your stories about what makes you a great director. If you have a problem with the use of "I did" leadership language you may use statements such as "My team launched the first solar rocket ship to Mars under $2B budget."

- Do not dismiss your true value because you are too close to recognize it. We often take for granted the things that we do well because we have been doing them for a long time and they come naturally to us. Many people struggle with understanding the special value of their value proposition because of this. If you are one of them, consider asking your network and professionals who know your work to help.

- Reflect where you want to go, not simply where you have been. Targeting how you can add value to board discussions and decision-making processes help position you with stakeholders for the opportunities that need your insights.

- Focus on your accomplishments, not your responsibilities. My son had the responsibility to make his bed every day—but that did not mean that he accomplished it. Tell what impact and successes you have had, not on the role of your job.

What to Include in Your Board Biography

- **Board service and experiences**
  List any corporate board-service experience. Highlight your responsibilities and accomplishments on these boards and any developments where you played a major role. You may briefly mention your services on nonprofit boards, though I would not spend a lot of time on them, if at all, because nonprofit board service is generally disregarded

for corporate board services. Include your experiences in a corporate boardroom. Have you presented to a corporate board, or have you regularly attended board meetings? Board members want to know that you understand boardroom etiquette and board responsibilities.

- **Major operating experience**

  Focus on narrating your operating experience that you have gained throughout your career. Summarize your career from the beginning to its current point, with an eye for operational experience. Emphasize your key skills, expertise, experiences, and knowledge.

- **Notable work experience**

  Add your work experience to your board biography narrative. Instead of simply listing company names and dates, describe major projects that you have taken up in your career. Tell a meaningful and engaging story of your career. Detail your role in these projects and how you helped them succeed. It is a good idea to emphasize your leadership roles and strategic contributions.

- **Business opportunities**

  Discuss the business opportunities that you have taken and how you followed through to success. Reading about your business opportunities helps others to better understand your potential and your ability to assess and navigate risk.

- **Roles on technical teams**

  Depending on the industry, it may be worth approaching your board biography from a technical point of view. While you avoid jargon and want to make sure that the board biography recipients can follow your board papers, you also want to make sure that your expertise shines through in all your board documents and communications.

- **Educational qualifications**

  It is essential to mention your educational qualifications in your board biography. Educational qualification is the cornerstone of your career and often an important factor considered by board candidate evaluators.

Appendix E features many sample board biographies. Feel free to use these as an inspiration. Appendix F features a template that you can use to start drafting your own board biography.

Why Is a Board Resume/CV Important?
How to Write It?

Your board resume/CV is an inventory that expands on the points in your board biography. It gives a factual account of your career progression and discusses in more depth your career experiences and states relevant facts to help the reader reach the unavoidable conclusion—that you are a good fit for her board.

Use your traditional resume as a place to start and tailor it in tone with the board audience in mind. Make sure that it complements and expands on your board profile and board biography.

A perfect board resume is based on the facts about your career. The goal is not to tell a story of your life but to strategically highlight your qualifications, skills, experience, expertise, and achievements. It should be a compelling inventory about the unique value that would you bring as a director.

A Few General Rules to Consider

- Jargon words and phrases are not helpful. For example, terms like "self-motivated" and "action-oriented" describe everyone at this level.
- Showcase your accomplishments using words such as "achieved" and "launched." Phrases like "responsible for" do not show your accomplishments. See a list of recommended words in the Appendix F.
- Add your previous experience, the details of the companies where you have worked, and your specific and measurable accomplishments.
- Also add details about your academic history and other professionally relevant value. This includes achievements, skills, expertise, experience, and knowledge.
- Of course, be sure to include your contact information so that others can get in touch with you.
- As always, your resume should be professional, impactful, clean, and clear. It should also be in PDF format, double-checked for typos, and with point size large enough to read.

- Make sure your board resume/CV is no more than two to three pages. If it seems too long to you, it is!
- Test your board resume/CV with other directors for their feedback.

One of the questions often asked is "How should I format my resume/ CV to present my skills and experience." Most senior executives have produced chronological resumes/CVs throughout their careers, which list their key achievements and experiences in chronological order. This is not the best route today. This kind of resume/CV can make it difficult for a reader to identify the value that you can bring to their company.

A hybrid approach is to have a board profile-type paragraph highlighting your major accomplishments and career experience as the top portion of the document to show your major qualifiers as a board candidate. Follow with a few bullet points documenting the accomplishments that you have summarized in the opening. There is no need to title this information as the "Summary" which just takes up space on the page. Follow this board profile with the chronological history of your career with company names, titles, and key accomplishments in those positions that helped lead to the overall company's success. These success measures typically document your role of increasing revenue and profitability, reducing costs, reducing risk, or documenting some other metric that had an overarching positive impact on each company.

Many candidates believe that more is better in outlining their career history. Nothing could be further from the truth. Your resume/CV is a summary of your roles and accomplishments that support your claim that you are qualified for a board seat. You must question the value of every piece of information that you include to determine if it strengthens your case.

Your resume/CV should be viewed as your template that you may need to tweak for each board opportunity. While your overall "wheelhouse" and value proposition typically stay close to your brand, providing more details on how those tie to a particular industry, company, product, or need is a smart approach.

Additional Tips about Your Board Bio and Resume/CV

Nancy Sheppard, my editor and contributor to this book, provides some additional insights on writing these documents as she has helped so many women go through the board journey process. She admits that it is often very difficult for many of them to sit down and do the actual writing. Many successful executives have not had to sell themselves for years—they have been promoted up in an organization—because they did a great job. She notes that those who know you may ask you to serve on a board because they have had one on one experience with you, but the majority of aspiring directors have to sell themselves, and these documents, including LinkedIn, are sales tools to get you in front of board decision makers.

She equates this phase of the journey of getting these "right" with the Go-to-Market approach. You are the product, and you need to get packaged to be a product that boards want to have.

- Your board biography and board resume/CV get scanned quickly (usually within two minutes) by a search firm, registry manager, CEO, or nominating committee, so the most important rule is to make it easy to see the value that you can bring as a director.

- Starting a board search plan without a well-thought-out board package is ill advised. Taking care to get it right is imperative. If you are not sure that your bio or resume/CV will make you attractive to boards that you expect to target, then this is one place that you should spend a few dollars to work with a specialist to assist you.

- Many executives put together an ineffective board resume/CV because they do not understand the differences between executive and board resumes. The job search methodology of merely listing job titles and responsibilities just does not work for boards.

- Candidates must clearly focus on what is relevant to a board. Your experiences should be linked to build a story matching your background with the needs of the role. Do not expect anyone but you to draw the lines between your accomplishments and their needs, the lines that demonstrate your fit and relevancy.

- Ideally, your board biography and resume/CV will be adapted for a board once you know their needs, but you will need to develop a generic biography and resume/CV for search firms and registries, and to complement your LinkedIn profile. If possible, identify your director capabilities and value proposition for your targeted boards. If you have a targeted board, review the current board listing to evaluate needed gaps in their skills and experience and highlight your own in these areas.

Here Are a Dozen Golden Rules When You Write Board Documents

1. Present what you will be able to do based upon what you have accomplished; do not just outline the experience and positions you have had.
2. Adopt director level thinking to highlight your value to a board.
3. Your value should be obvious in the first half of page one.
4. Kick off with a profile summary, bringing together your unique capabilities in a short paragraph or two.
5. Follow the summary with the core skills that tie in with those required by the board target.
6. Show that you are a thought leader in one or more of your stated expertise areas.
7. Show key accomplishments with clear metrics that show the scale of your experiences.
8. Demonstrate that you can summarize a lengthy career in a succinct presentation.
9. Validate that you understand and will embrace a governance role (you do not own or execute the activity) vs. a management role.
10. Write in a straightforward, factual, and direct style yet with enough of a story to provide insights into how you will show up in the boardroom.
11. Ensure board skill sets of counseling and advising, and ideal committee roles are apparent.
12. Listing years of service or accomplishments in past positions (especially over 10 years ago) are much less important than what you can bring now. Your most recent experience is the *most* relevant, so make it the focus.

Appendix E features sample board biographies and resumes that you can use to start drafting your own board resume.

How to Build Relationships to Become a Director?

Finding the right board position requires active and intentional relationship building. This can be compared to growing a crop. You need to plant the seeds, cultivate them with care, and then harvest the fruits of your labor. Intentional strategy, flawless execution, and good timing are important.

You must build your network to achieve success as a director before and after you join a board. And your network must be both deep and wide to help you join a board and succeed as a director. You must actively network and build authentic, long-lasting relationships to become a director. Here are some ways to cultivate relationships that can help you identify or even connect you to board opportunities:

- **Embrace the notion that building a director-ready network is a time-consuming process**
  Meet professionals in person at corporate gatherings, meetings, and conferences. Do not forget to also "meet" individuals through social media platforms such as LinkedIn and Twitter. Branding yourself on social media for a board seat needs to be focused with a very professional approach. This is a public record of you, and board members will review your social media presence when doing their due diligence on you. Do not make the mistake of using these to be known as something other than the type of person a board would want their company to be identified with. We have seen recently how activities from long ago come back to haunt executives and politicians. Clear out your social media of anything that would be less than prudent.

  Do not be afraid to ask for help creating a strong, director-ready network. Try to meet professionals who have been in business for a long time and have achieved a lot of experience, skills, networking, expertise, and knowledge. They may be helpful in sharing their insights, introducing you to their network, and ultimately helping you to join a board.

- **Create a process to network systematically and intentionally**

To become a director, you must network systematically and intentionally. You must understand the value of your network. Create a system to strategically and periodically meet, contact, and keep in touch with people who can bring you closer to your goal. For example, you can make it a goal to reach out to a specific number of contacts on LinkedIn per week or attend at least three networking events per month. Make sure you also have a way to keep track of all your new contacts. Do not lose opportunities by simply forgetting to follow up or keep in touch with a valuable contact!

- **Prioritize networking with directors, chairs, and board influencers and CEOs first**

  Becoming a director is both a contacts game and a numbers game. Be sure that your professional network includes directors, chairs, and CEOs. More than 70% of positions are filled through their recommendations. Also, make sure that all kinds of other professionals—especially those that interact or assist boards—including lawyers, bankers, accountants, consultants, venture capitalists and PE partners and some talent directors, and numerous others are part of your network. Keep in mind that building a network takes time and that director-ready networks are both deep and wide.

- **Strategically expand your network**

  Board service is all about relationships. Aim to regularly meet several relevant professionals from the industry that you are targeting. You should network with professionals who are respected in the industry or have connections to boards. To do this, you will need to attend relevant social gatherings, conferences, meetings, and other networking events. At these events, be sure to ask for introductions. To get an introduction, contact people in your network or even those who are a few degrees removed.

  You may have to contact professionals whom you have never met before, have only met briefly, or have not spoken to in a while. Although this may be uncomfortable, you need to persist and connect with them on a regular basis. Show genuine interest in the person and what they do. Although not every new contact will lead to a board opportunity, the connections you make now will certainly serve you well when you are a director.

You may also seek out recruiters who work with corporate boards or help boards find new candidates, industry influencers, and numerous others. You never know where your board opportunities will come from!

- **Intentionally participate in social media to showcase your skills, expertise, and knowledge**

  Social media is an extension of your board pitch, board biography, and board resume/CV. LinkedIn is a great place to start for many industries. As discussed, be sure to create a comprehensive profile on LinkedIn and engage regularly. It is customary for companies to check out your LinkedIn profile and Google your name well before they initially contact you about a director opportunity. LinkedIn is also a great place to meet new professionals, including directors, chair persons, CEOs, founders, service providers, and numerous others.

- **Regularly maintain quality, authentic relationships**

  A professional relationship is different from a personal relationship. To build up a professional relationship consider following the steps below:

  - Publishing articles, blogs, papers, and books can help you to get noticed and cement your position as an influencer and leader in your industry. Consider sharing your knowledge and resources on LinkedIn.

  - Join board LinkedIn groups, and comment, publish, and reach out to members on these director and CEO networks.

  - Attending conferences, seminars, and meetups is a great way to network and stay on the top of your industry. Consider sharing your attendance and learnings on LinkedIn.

  - If you are involved in any organizations or projects, it may be a good idea to supplement your LinkedIn profile to paint a more complete picture of yourself as a prospective director.

  - Thoughtfully comment and engage with other professionals on LinkedIn.

- Aim to be helpful to others on LinkedIn either by sharing information or networks with others.

- Be a good listener. Nobody wants to feel patronized or used. Listen to what they are saying and ask questions to show interest. This is a valuable way to learn information about your target industry, company, corporate board of directors, and executives.

- In preparation, research the professional that you are about to meet and her company. You can make a deeper connection if you can identify some common interests, mutual acquaintances, or background to discuss.

- Consistently be helpful, generous, relevant, and timely in your offers, comments, and interactions. You can be persistent without being annoying. Make sure that you offer to assist with the other person's goals as well—you may find that you can both help each other.

- Be responsive. As you build relationships, other professionals will ask you for introductions or give invitations to speak. While you do not have to accept everything, you can acknowledge the request and ways that you can assist, even if it is only a word of support or a "like" on social media.

- Share your specific goals and aspirations to become a director and ask for specific ways that they can be helpful to you. Many professionals are happy to help others but are not sure how. If you can identify specific ways that they can help, you can take the pressure off.

Appendix A provides a *Networking Plan* worksheet that you can use to visualize and strategize as you build a director-ready network.

What Are the Practical Strategies to Join Your First Board Soon?

Starting a career as a director can fuel your future by giving you more interesting opportunities. However, not every open board seat will be right for you. You must join a company that will complement your specific skills and management power. Yet many prospective and current directors agree that finding a first board opportunity is especially challenging. Here are some suggestions to help you with finding and enjoying your first board opportunity:

- **Search broadly**
  It is intuitive to look for a board position in an industry where you have at least some experience. Consider searching for opportunities in adjacent or complementary industries as well. For example, the industries of your vendors or suppliers may offer a perfect place for your board service.

- **Articulate your value fit clearly, consistently, and often**
  Articulate what unique value that you will bring to a board. This can help you identify a board where you will be the best fit. You will most likely thrive on a board where your value fills a gap or provides a new perspective.

- **Research and evaluate potential target companies**
  Where is the company in its development? What challenges does the company face? Is the company expanding internationally? Is it involved in M&A? Where is it financially? Does it need financing? Is it winding down or is it considering filing for bankruptcy? Is your target company small or large? Is it private or public? Is it a startup? Is your target company under close government investigation? Does it deal with regulators often? After researching the company, evaluate how this information fits into your specific corporate board brand. Do your skills, experience, expertise, and knowledge position you to be helpful to your target companies? If so, how? You can add more value if you have had experience handling the challenges and opportunities that the company currently has.

- **Get to know activist investors**
  Get to know activist investors. While this was not an advisable practice in the past, the culture and expectations have changed. An activist investor is an individual or group that purchases large numbers of a public company's shares or tries to obtain seats on the company's board with the goal of making a major change in the

company. Activist investors may be looking for qualified director candidates that can be placed on a board. Before accepting a position from an activist investor, make sure that you understand the specific activist investor, what motivates them, what outcome they want, and why they are interested in you for their target board.

- **Leverage your angel investor experience**
Angel investors (or "angels") provide a startup or early stage company with the required funds to start a business. Through the entire process, the role of an angel investor is vital. They offer the requisite capital with particular "terms and conditions" as the basis for their investment. As they are providing capital, they may also work as a mentor for a startup business.

  After diligence and investing, angels may informally or formally advise founders on numerous issues. Depending on their interest, expertise, skills, experience, and knowledge, investors may play the role of a board observer. Although they may not have voting rights to make any major decision for the business, their opinion is highly valued. Occasionally, an angel investor may even join the startup's director.

  If you have experience as an angel investor, you can translate your skills to board service. When discussing your angel investing experience, highlight any impact you have made on a startup's long-term strategy and success. Also emphasize any operational experience that you may have gained. Of course, if you have held a role on the startup's board of directors or advisory board, this experience can also be leveraged to gain a position on other boards.

- **Consider serving on a prominent nonprofit board of directors**
You can also start with a nonprofit board of directors. Although these opportunities may be very different from corporate board opportunities, they can present great opportunities to learn, network, and sharpen corporate governance skills, and get started with board service—all the while you help a cause you care about.

  Keep in mind, the most powerful reason to join a nonprofit board is to serve in pursuit of your strong passion, not as a mere stepping stone on the way to a corporate board. There may also be other opportunities where you can start your for-profit board journey that may be more effective.

Although a nonprofit board may be the obvious choice for starting your board journey, it is important to only take that route if you are truly passionate about the cause. Nonprofit board service is a highly important endeavor, not just as a stepping stone to a larger for-profit board service goal. If you are looking for a more appropriate, and perhaps even more advantageous "starter board," look at opportunities falling into one of the following four categories. Not only will you give yourself a great jumpstart for your for-profit board-service journey, but you will also ensure that you are contributing to the best of your ability.

- **Ask your employer for help**

  Many companies struggle to retain top executives because the opportunities to grow or advance may not be apparent when you are one of the most senior professionals in the organization. Consider asking your CEO, chairperson, and directors to help you become a director. Explain to them how this new challenge will benefit the company, increase your learning, and facilitate your loyalty to the company. Involving your employer to help you secure your first director opportunity is a pro move that is highly effective, and very few professionals utilize it. Ask your company to pay for your attendance at board training institutes, conferences or a certification program, and/or your membership in a board-readiness program.

- **Consider serving on a subsidiary board of your employer**

  If you work for a company that acquires other companies, has subsidiaries, or has other related businesses, and you are in a senior position, consider asking to serve on a board of directors of one of those related businesses. This is another way to enlist your current employer into helping you become a director. Moreover, it is a relatively safe way to get into board service because you are already familiar with the business, industry, and main stakeholders. The decision makers may be excited that you have volunteered for an extra assignment. They may also be glad to promote you or give you this recognition when there may not be other obvious opportunities to do so.

- **Consider serving on a small or private company**

  Do not go for the big, public Fortune 500 companies at the initial stage of your board journey. Consider intentionally growing your board career over time. When you start out, it may be a good idea to begin your board service with a private company or a small public company. Then, as you gain skills, confidence, expertise, network, experience, and knowledge, you can consider whether you have the time, energy, and interest to pursue larger, more high-profile public boards.

- **Consider serving on a foreign company's board**

  Many companies abroad operate or do business in the United States or your country. They often prefer for their prospective directors to (in addition to having substantive expertise in the industry) know the U.S. or other markets or understand the local industries, customs, or regulatory landscapes.

  Moreover, many companies outside of the United States operate in jurisdictions that have explicit diversity requirements; for example, France requires 30 percent of its public directors to be women. Therefore, these foreign companies may cast a very broad net and be willing to recruit professionals outside of their country when they fill their boards. Joining a foreign private or public company board is an excellent opportunity to network, learn about your industry globally, and build a director portfolio.

- **Consider serving on a startup board**

  A startup is a new business that is still being built. For new entrepreneurs, starting their own company is a huge undertaking. Most of them think that a startup board is not of importance, at least for the groundbreaking process. Over time, many startups that survive the first few years may rethink this position as they educate themselves about their industry, their business, and the value that directors bring.

  Often, the need for a board arises if there is an investor who demands that a board be formed. A board may also become necessary if an entrepreneur wants to address certain needs of her company. The professionals an entrepreneur chooses for her board are critical to her business' performance. As time progresses, she may need to involve more people with certain expertise, knowledge, or experience.

Executives, senior management officers, former regulators, and industry leaders are among the people who may be included on a startup's board of directors. They may become key decision makers and even be involved hand-on in a startup. Startup boards often offer valuable professional opportunities and are a great way to start your board journey. They are an excellent way to network, learn more about different industries, and build a successful record of guiding businesses through a critical stage. Just make sure that you are clear about the expectations and what you are willing to do for the startup board to be helpful.

- **Consider serving on an advisory board (aka council)**
Advisory boards exist to offer fine expertise to other boards or executives such as the CEO. Advisory boards also complement other functional areas of the organization, such as the management team or task forces. For many startup ventures, advisory boards are often highly prioritized. A well-managed and well-structured advisory board can enhance the bandwidth and ensure the right outcome for an organization.

These are usually non-governing boards with no fiduciary duty. Because of this, some do not agree that advisory boards should be called boards. Even if you prefer to call them "councils" instead of boards, these opportunities still merit consideration. Advisory boards often offer valuable professional opportunities and are a great way to start your board journey. They can be a good first introduction to corporate board service. However, because advisory boards can be so variable, if you join one, consider being clear about the expectations and what you will be able to contribute.

CHAPTER 6

Who Can Join a Corporate Board?

Board service is becoming an increasingly attractive career option. Although the traditional director is an ex-CEO or other high-level executive, professionals from all fields can leverage their skills to earn a board position. This chapter outlines how various professionals, such as entrepreneurs, academics, financial professionals, private equity professionals, engineers and other technical professionals, and lawyers can contribute to a board. Finally, this chapter also addresses the myth of being too young or too old to become a director.

The main takeaway from this chapter is that diversity of thought is a plus for all boards and having a diverse background may be useful for a prospective director. As the general rule, there is no objectively perfect board or a perfect director. There are, however, certain boards and directors that are a perfect match.

Do Academics Qualify to Serve on a Board?

Academics may play a role on a board. A reputable, well-known, influential academic serving on a corporate board of directors tells a lot about a company and its prestige and reputation. It is important for a company to include directors who deeply understand the subject matter that is core to the business.

Academic leaders who have any entrepreneurial experience, who understand real-world business outside the academic context, and who have important and relevant subject-matter expertise may be very attractive to the board of directors. An academic may bring the following qualities to a corporate board of directors:

- **Strategic skills**
  A board is always in need of new strategies to take the business to the next level. Generally, most boards are looking for problem-solving skills, leadership qualities, strategic thinking skills, and an industry understanding. Depending on one's individual experience and interests, an academic may already have these strategic skills and will be able to convey the depth of company's and its board's expertise in a certain, often niche, subject matter.

- **Interpersonal skills and professional judgment**
  A board also wants a professional with good interpersonal skills and good professional judgment. Depending on their experiences and focus, some academics may excel in discussing important and controversial topics and objectively analyzing evidence to find the right answer. Academics may also excel at maintaining transparency in professional relationships and collective undertakings.

- **Diversity of thought**
  Diversity of thought is an asset for a board. Academics may bring much-needed diversity to a board as well as a rigorous hypothesis testing methodology. They can also help the company evaluate different viewpoints toward relevant issues, strengthening its core operations.

- **Experiences on the cutting edge of research**
  Usually, companies look for experienced and mature directors, with an excellent amount of experience in the same industry. Academics can have skills, experience, expertise, and knowledge in areas where they have spent a lifetime researching, teaching, and publishing. In fact, they may be on a cutting edge of the research which may be a substantial advantage in more experimental, new, or science-driven industries.

Do Entrepreneurs Qualify to Serve on a Board?

Entrepreneurs may be qualified to serve on a board. It is essential that an entrepreneur board candidate has enough experience operating a business, often in a relevant or adjacent industry. An entrepreneur may bring the following qualities to a corporate board of directors:

- **Good business judgment**
  Good business judgment is the prime skill of every director. An entrepreneur's board profile, biography, and resume/CV often demonstrate a track record of hiring good people, making sound business decisions, having industry knowledge and deep important relationships, as well as overall good judgment.
- **Knowledge and skills**
  Another essential point is that an entrepreneur should be knowledgeable about relevant trends, practices, key stakeholders, and ethics. Entrepreneurs often demonstrate a strategic and technical point of view. They display a track record of handling certain important situations and milestone events (such as overseas expansion) successfully and systematically. An experienced entrepreneur is most likely to have good judgment skills and great knowledge.
- **Industry dedication and insights**
  If an entrepreneur is highly attracted toward working in this company's field, chances are high that they can produce productive positive results. Being passionate about your work is the key to success. An entrepreneur will often demonstrate a deep passion and long-term commitment to an industry.
- **Unwavering focus**
  Entrepreneurs often devote significant time and effort to the organization. Many professionals are interested in getting on a board but do not have enough time to be truly focused on a new organization. It is essential that every director makes a serious time commitment to their organization. An entrepreneur is often able to demonstrate unwavering focus and interest in their organizations' success.

Do Professionals with Financial Backgrounds Qualify to Serve on Boards?

Professionals with backgrounds in finance are sought after for boards. Some companies even prefer candidates who are qualified "finance experts." In any event, accounting and finance are the language that companies speak, and professionals who are fluent in these areas are generally highly desirable.

Financial education and experience in the industry where the target company operates are very important. When choosing a director with financial expertise, companies often look for the following:

- **Work experience**

   Excellent work experience is important, especially in the relevant industry. Companies prefer to hire directors with a deep understanding of specific and relevant financial issues. Companies, especially public companies, have historically preferred on boards working CEOs or chief financial officers (CFOs), especially those from Fortune 500 companies.

   Have you held titles such as CFO, treasurer, vice president of finance, director of finance, director of accounting, director of financial reporting, corporate controller, controller, divisional controller, or a similar title? Have you dealt with tax, compliance, generally accepted accounting principles, financials, modeling, budget, treasury, costs, Securities and Exchange Commission (SEC) and other regulators, tariffs, audit, and similar issues? If so, make sure that your board profile, board resume/CV, and board biography indicate the size of the budget that you managed, transactions that you led, and milestones that you achieved. Include this information in the beginning where it can be easily found.

- **Financial education**

   Relevant and current financial education, training, and credentials are important. Be sure to emphasize your finance and accounting-related credentials, certifications, and coursework. Also highlight any specific educational or membership milestones. For example, if you are a certified public accountant (CPA) that is highly relevant information.

- **Continue your education**

   Keep yourself updated about new financial requirements, especially those that affect your industry or companies. Consider attending industry events that focus on finance and accounting, especially in your industry. Network and keep in touch with CPAs and other finance and accounting professionals. Make sure you read financial literature including books, newspapers, academic papers, industry white papers, and blogs. This way you can keep your hand on the pulse and stay conversant about important financial issues.

Do Private Equity Professionals Qualify to Serve on Boards?

Private equity professionals can be valuable prospective directors for many reasons such as the following:

- **Understanding financials and operational mastery**
  Private equity professionals are sophisticated about finance, accounting, and operations. Therefore, they may be valuable prospective directors, especially if they have relevant industry experience. They may be very helpful in advising the board about the best ways to raise money, reduce operational costs, and minimize related risk. They are also strategic in their thinking and execution. Their experiences are deeply rooted in the operational realities of a business.
- **Mastery and management of investments**
  Private equity professionals may be well positioned to help companies that are involved in investments because they may have helpful insights, experiences, and relationships. For example, they can help manage expectations about expected returns or help structure investments. They may also be able to monitor company investments to ensure that their performances meet management's expectations. Finally, private equity professionals can be instrumental in helping the board to structure its strategy for acquiring or selling various assets.
- **Superb experience, expertise, and training**
  Private equity professionals often go through rigorous training process consisting of valuable experiences and education. Therefore, many private equity professionals consistently have stellar education, impressive experiences, and a track record of impact. Moreover, on-the-job training often contributes to their superb experience, expertise, and a high degree of financial literacy.

Do Engineers and Other Technical Professionals Qualify to Serve on Boards?

It is helpful for engineers and other technical professionals to be skilled in the arts and sciences that the target company practices to at least some extent. In addition to their substantive technical skills, engineers and other technical professionals may bring other value to a corporate board of directors.

- **Innovative ideas**
  When engineers and other technical professionals serve on a board, they may be instrumental in ensuring that the organization is moving with the times by bringing in new product or manufacturing ideas to benefit both prospective and existing customers. This helps a company stay innovative, relevant, and competitive. It also helps companies recruit and retain technical and product talent.
- **Quantitative skills**
  As expected, engineers and other technical professionals are often strong in mathematics and science. This means that they also tend to be very good at understanding product-related or research-related quantitative information. They also tend to understand financial and accounting information and trends, be able to comprehend a large volume of quantitative data, and systematically ask relevant questions.
- **Practical experience of building desirable product and services**
  Engineers and other technical professionals often have education, training, skills, experience, knowledge, and expertise in building products and finding product-market fit. They may be useful to have on a corporate board of directors when a company considers launching a new product offering, changing an existing product offering, expanding its product offering to other geographies, acquiring other products to add to its portfolio, or dealing with technical regulators such as the US Food and Drug Administration.
- **Experience researching and building products**
  Engineers and technical professionals who have worked their way up to becoming a director are often proactive in nature and have

experience listening to customer feedback. They often have the knowledge and technical know-how to spot a problem and have it tackled in a professional way before it will even surface. They can also help the company listen and interpret customer feedback.

What Experiences Can Lawyers Bring to a Board?

There has been a continued argument about whether lawyers should be part of a board of directors or not. Lawyers can bring many experiences and skills to corporate boards of directors:

- **Influencing others and independence**
  Lawyers spend their careers advising and influencing others on specific issues and risks which may be affecting their companies. They give their independent advice on the options that a business may have. A lawyer can transfer these skills to board service and be a useful voice of reason for a board. Showing their experience in managing a business sector can be very important.

- **Conflict resolutions skills**
  Disputes, legal or otherwise, arise for all companies. For some, they may even be routine. Lawyers are generally good at strategically managing and advising boards of directors about navigating risks at various stages of conflict. Lawyers may add value to businesses that have a high conflict or litigation risk.

- **Risk-management experience**
  Lawyers often have experiences managing risks related to procurement, contracts, patents, property, government regulations, international expansion, mergers and acquisitions, initial public offering , and numerous other areas. Depending on their experience, they may also have broad exposure and management experience in legal and business issues. This can help lawyers provide a useful perspective to boards.

- **Great communication skills**
  Lawyers spend a lifetime perfecting their communication skills in many settings and circumstances. They negotiate, mediate, argue, influence, educate, relate, advocate, and strategically communicate throughout their careers, all of which are an asset for a board.

- **Analytical skills**

  Lawyers are skilled at deliberately learning, analyzing, and inter-preting various situations and risks, as well as making decisions and acting upon these learnings and insights. These are very helpful qualities for directors. A lawyer on a board can help to structure a discussion, assist in decision making, and act in a more logical and systematic way.

- **Researching skills**

  Proper research is the hallmark of legal education and practice. It is an essential foundation for managing risks and coping with uncertainty. Lawyers can help a board to research and educate themselves better. They are skilled at making sense of a volume of information, identifying missing information, and finding ways to fill in the gaps systematically. They can also be helpful in framing and reframing questions for a board to focus on.

- **Problem-solving skills**

  Attorneys are experts at solving problems strategically and inten-tionally. The following skills are helpful for many problem-solving challenges:

- Attorneys possess substantial intellectual qualities and skills to complement the other existing corporate directors.
- They are comfortable handling the social and intellectual complex-ity of the corporate boardroom.
- They can masterfully navigate major perspectives, legal issues, and ethical dilemmas.
- Lawyers have the skills to analyze and address business challenges.
- They can contribute useful insights and bring diversity to board-room debates.
- Lawyers can facilitate crucial decision making in the boardroom.
- Lawyers are trained and experienced in absorbing and analyzing large volumes of information and documents.

What Age Is Too Old to Serve on a Board?

Historically, the average age of a corporate director is a little over sixty. To an extent this makes sense. Many companies want professionals with a successful career full of achievements, skills, experience, expertise, and knowledge to serve on their corporate boards. For most directors, especially at public companies, board service is an appropriate career move after a successful and thriving professional career, often in the same industry as the company where they serve.

The age of directors (and their term limits) is a much-discussed topic in the corporate world today. Ultimately, just like everyone else, seasoned professionals must articulate the answers to two fundamental questions: What unique value do they bring to a corporate board of directors, and what will they do to stay relevant?

Professionals with longer careers tend to have a larger wealth of education, training, experience, expertise, achievement, and knowledge that helps them to articulate their unique value proposition for a corporate board of directors. They also tend to have a wider and deeper network of professional contacts and might have a historic perspective on a company or industry.

These professionals also tend to a have a longer track record. They often command respect due to their achievements and age. Historically, some companies may consider age as an asset for corporate boards because age highly correlates with the attributes that many companies seek.

Yet every professional, of any age, who wants to serve on a board of directors must be able to articulate how they will stay relevant in an industry that may be changing quickly. How will you help promote new thoughts and understand new trends? How will you stay on top of your industry and profession? What classes or experiences will you seek? What books and periodicals will you read? What experts will you use to help you stay up to date? How will you educate yourself about new technologies, developments, and trends?

Regardless of age, it is important to understand your responsibility to stay relevant, active, and educated. While there may be a correlation with age, age is a red herring that must be ignored in favor of evaluating each candidate's qualifications a fit. The average age of larger public company boards has increased in the last few years. Unlike most jobs, the ages of board members (and key executives of SEC-reporting companies) are public information. Some boards have age limits, which has been increasing as well. There are arguments in favor of, and in opposition to, the policy of retiring directors because of their age just as there are for the use of term limits.

What Age Is Too Young to Serve on a Board?

This is the era of new thoughts, technology, and ideas, which has completely dominated the business world in the last few decades. Younger professionals are increasingly present on boards because they bring fresh ideas, start new trends, can connect with a company's customers, understand the digital world, and help overcome the boring persistence of old ideas and the status quo.

Younger directors can enrich a board with their new thoughts and ideas. They can fill the potential gaps of a growing business. As a young professional, your hunger, passion, and creativity will help you add fuel to your board journey.

One of the secrets of a successful board is diversity of thought. A well-balanced board with different points of view, ages, experiences, strategies, opinions, and voices can better reach business goals. And many boards are becoming more open minded about young board candidates.

Consider approaching a board service strategically and early. While it can be very daunting to start a career as a director, especially at a young age, it may be a prudent approach because it may ultimately help your build you career and start preparing for board service early.

For example, serving on a board may be an amazing experience that goes along with (not after) your career. It may increase and enrich your opportunities, knowledge, skills, experience, visibility, and network. As a young director consider these strategies to position yourself to serve on a corporate board relatively early in your career:

- **Emphasize fresh ideas, new approaches, emerging industries, and cutting-edge technology**

  In articulating your board value proposition, consider emphasizing your fresh ideas, new approaches, experience in emerging industries, and knowledge of cutting-edge technologies. Do you know about emerging market trends that many people miss? Do you understand how new technology will impact the industry, company, products, disciplines, consumer behavior, regulations, or supply chain? Are you fluent in new, emerging, and hot technologies, such as Internet of Things, artificial intelligence, virtual reality, or blockchain? Make sure that you develop deep expertise in these new and exciting areas.

- **Develop broad thinking and leadership skills**

    Boards generally focus on planning and strategy, not minutiae or day-to-day operations. Seek experiences and assignments with broad roles, be able to think strategically, and lead. Routinely ask yourself: Do my current opportunities give me the full picture? Am I progressing in developing my skills? Do I routinely participate in setting strategy? Am I part of the P&L discussion? Am I responsible for a sizable budget? If you sense that your current role is not preparing you for board service, seek out new projects or even employment that connect you with more strategic, leadership roles.

- **Actively and intentionally consider how board service may enhance your career today**

    Becoming a director early will provide you with learning, growth, expertise, experience, and networking opportunities that will help your career as well. Consider educating yourself about the richness of board opportunities—nonprofit, startup, family businesses, private companies, public companies, and Fortune 500.

    Understand that between nonprofit and Fortune 500 boards, there is a rich middle ground of opportunities that most professionals completely miss. Appreciate how these opportunities are different, where you can provide value, and how they can go along with your career. Board opportunities of all kinds may help you grow your career, boost your leadership skills, increase your expertise, provide new challenges, present opportunities to give back, and expand your network.

- **Intentionally grow your network deep and wide early**

    You are never too young to strategically grow your network. You want to make sure that your network is vast, composed of people from various disciplines, backgrounds, and perspectives. Consider including current directors, chairpersons, CEOs, executives, founders, vice-presidents, industry influencers, subject-matter leaders, and numerous other professionals who work with boards of directors. This will give you a head start on your board journey.

- **Embrace the digital age and new technologies**

  The digital age is here. The Internet offers a wealth of opportunities to learn, acquire skills, and expand your network. Take advantage of the numerous social platforms to start building your professional reputation early. What is your digital reputation? What are you known for? Do you regularly share content consistent with your reputation and values? Are you becoming an expert in a certain subject matter, industry, or geography?

- **Develop an international perspective and presence**

  In the increasingly global economy, a genuine understanding of international culture, market, environment, technology, entertainment, and trends is valuable. It also takes time to develop these qualities and skills. Consider developing your world intelligence quotient (IQ) and worldview early. Seek out jobs and assignment with international responsibilities, network with peers in your global company, travel, learn about markets, and get involved in international organizations and nongovernmental organizations.

Appendix A features a *Board-Ready Thought Leader* worksheet that you can use to plan your board readiness at any stage of your career.

CHAPTER 7

Due Diligence: How to Join the Right Board, Grow Professionally, and Safeguard Your Director Reputation

Becoming a director is a massive commitment. It is essential to make sure the specific board opportunity you are eyeing is right for you and your future. Be sure to do your due diligence to identify any issues that you may face as a director at a specific company. Ultimately, due diligence can help you decide whether a specific board position is right for you. This chapter explains how to research information about companies as well as their boards and executives, how to identify red flags, and how to evaluate the information you uncover.

What Is a Good and Systematic Approach to Due Diligence?

It is important to research a company before agreeing to join as a director. While there are many approaches you can follow, it is important to have a plan and review all information systematically. One way to do so effectively and deliberately is to consider different sources of information produced inside and outside of the company.

- **Inside sources of information**
  Start with inside information, the information that companies generate themselves. Companies generate quantitative and qualitative information, both of which could be helpful in researching your target companies and preparing for interviews.

These sources fall into two categories: quantitative and qualitative. It is important to review both.

Quantitative inside information includes financial statements, financial statement footnotes, stock valuation, and similar information. This quantitative inside information tells a story, and it is important to understand it. Qualitative inside information includes financial statements, statements made when attending or listening to conference calls, and material on the company's website such as investor packets and presentations. This qualitative information provides insights and color.

One way to access the important inside information is to review a company's Securities and Exchange Commission (SEC) filings (if you are conducting due diligence on a public company). To understand the quantitative and qualitative inside information, the SEC filings may be a good place to gather information. Look for the presentation consistency and work style of the company. Research one or more types of information like how they face questions, how they answer these questions in different ways over time, trustworthiness, and whether their performance proves their statements.

- **Outside sources of information**
  In addition, it is also important to review outside sources of information or that which was not produced by the company. There are many sources of outside information to consider.
- Consider asking people in your network, preferably in person, their opinion on the company. Generally, people do not like to put qualified or negative information in emails. People in your network will be more forthcoming on the phone or in person.
- Message boards like Yahoo can be a great resource. Message boards can help you understand trends. Customers, clients, and vendors also post complaints on various boards.
- Another great way to get information about a company is analyst reports. When you are interviewing with a company, ask for the analyst's reports. Look for the original reports. Also, consider locating analyst reports on your own.

- Seeking Alpha and the Motley Fool, Crunchbase reports are other great outside sources.
- Of course, Google is your friend. You never know what you will find by doing a Google search!

What Information to Consider in Due Diligence of a Company?

When conducting due diligence of a company, you may find yourself swimming in a sea of information. Categorizing and paying attention to certain information may help you to focus on important elements of the company's narrative.

- **General information about the company**
  Consider researching the company thoroughly. Understand its assets, products, and services. Analyze the company's financial statements, stated objectives, and results to get further color about the business and its health. Get to know company business structure. Who owns what percentage? Where is the company looking to expend? What is the growth trajectory? Do they use distributors or sell directly to consumers or other businesses? Understand the competitive landscape and unique opportunities and challenges.
- **Goals and strategies**
  Companies frame goals every few years in association to fulfill their main, long-term objective. To analyze the performance and the success of an organization, you must understand the company's goals. Then you can identify specific projects that the company is working on and the strategies it is considering. Success or failure of the company in certain scenarios can also be noted.
- **Analyze the potential of the board of directors and the CEO**
  Analyzing the potential of the current directors and the chief executive officer (CEO) of the company will help you evaluate the potential success and the scope of working for the organization. The CEO and the directors are the core members of the organization. Decision making and overall strategy are explicitly dependent

on them. Assess the qualities of the CEO and directors, and their skills at managing the organization. How long have the CEO and each director been with the company? What is their backstory? Is there a succession plan? Has the CEO been reviewed annually?

- **Company's milestone events**
  Is the company going through or will soon be going through milestone events? Initial public offering? Mergers and acquisitions? Lawsuits? Restructuring? Bankruptcy? Additional commitments? Director training? Annual meetings or retreats? Social events? Are you expected to participate as an ambassador at these social events?

- **Values and perceptions**
  Investigate what it is like to work at the company. Specifically, analyze the values and perceptions the company follows and passes on to its employees. Research the professional, ethical, and legal principles of the company (or those that are missing from the company). Information from people with first-hand experience is most valuable. Employees of the company can be asked for their reviews.

- **Work environment**
  Investigate the company's work environment. What type of work environment does the organization offer? Is it good or bad? Are employees productive? Are they inspired about the company's mission and values? Research these questions. The work environment is a prime influencing characteristic for recruitment and the company image.

What Are the Due Diligence Red Flags?

Consider going through intensive due diligence before joining a board. Identifying red flags now will help you be successful in the future and guard your reputation. Here is where to look for red flags and the places that the board of directors has marked to improve or change:

- **Look for random and systematic risks**
  Directors must identify the flaws and risks that can develop into hazardous issues for their companies. You can use your network to find out about the current incidents and status of the company.

- **Watch out for auditor changes**

  Another red flag is when a company changes its auditor. An auditor is responsible for making the annual data audit of a company.

- **Pay attention to procedures and policies**

  The board is responsible for making policies for its organization or company. Boards must have all the information about the policies and different procedures of the company. Each director must read through them carefully and approve each policy before proceeding. There are various types of policies, such as policies for social media, emergency planning, acceptance of gifts, Sarbanes–Oxley compliance, and more. Directors also need to identify the reason for missing policies. Do the regulations not exist, or are the policies still under cover? They should have all this information.

- **Pay attention to board meetings**

  When do regular board meetings for a company normally take place? Are there any special board meetings? Has the frequency of these meetings increased? If so, why? Are all directors and executive staff of the company present at the meeting? If not, what is the reason? What is the normal source of information for the board? Is the board dependent on just one source to provide information, or is the board proactively educating its members using a variety of sources?

- **Pay attention to financial information**

  Of course, it is critical to understand a company's past and current financials. Financial statements should be examined. Remember, accounting and finance are the language of business. Understanding financials helps you see the full picture of a company. Have the right financial reports been sent on time? Have they been viewed by all the directors? Each director should be able to understand the statement in a board meeting. Is there any accounting method which can be only understood by the members of your finance department? Is there a responsible audit department for the company? Is there a departmental and organizational budget of the organization? Are the directors receiving timely reports on that budget?

How to Conduct Due Diligence on a Startup (or a Private Company) before Joining Its Board?

Joining a startup's or any private company's board of directors or advisory board may be very risky because a lot of the information may be private and not readily available. Unlike public companies that must disclose a certain amount of information, many private companies keep a lot of information to themselves. They are effectively black boxes to outsiders.

Due diligence is an effective process to identify the major risks of being involved with these types of boards. If a prospective startup investor, director, or advisory board member does not like everything they uncover in the due diligence process, they can take appropriate action. This can range from suggesting a risk mitigation to the company, backing out of the investment, or declining an offer to join as a director or advisory board member.

Due diligence is a straightforward process that may sound overwhelming if you do not have an accounting or legal background. It is now more standardized. What follows is a list of items to look for and request when you are conducting a due diligence on a startup (or private company):

- **Overview on client acquisition channels**
  It is helpful to request an overview of the company's prospective customers and the lead funnel, along with information on the costs of customer acquisition. If you have access to a good report or case studies of potential customers, it may be a good idea to review these as well. Add a complete customer's list in the pipeline of the company's recent sales.
- **Spreadsheet on key metrics**
  Consider reviewing key metrics, which your investors may ask for during the process of fundraising. For example, be sure to understand the company's users, revenue, cost of customer acquisition, rates of growth, lifetime value, runway, burn rate, and all the other core metrics of the company that you are following.
- **Financial projections**
  It is a good idea to understand a company's financial plan for the next 3 years. What is a clear and expected financial scenario for the

future of the company? Just like how investors carefully examine projections in due diligence, potential startup directors or advisory directors should engage in a similar exercise on a smaller scale.

- **Financial and strategic reports**
  Before joining a startup board of directors or advisory board consider reviewing financial and strategic reports of the company with the details of every director and other key people such as stockholders and vendors.

- **Key legal papers**
  Consider reviewing key legal documents from foreign and domestic jurisdictions for the company such as incorporation, leases, assets, taxes, locations of employees, and others.

- **Website and press releases**
  It is a good idea to review all the recent news, press releases, and website details. Be sure to Google the company. See what you can find. Have others written about the company, CEO, board, product, or services? Have you read the reviews? What about board discussions? It is definitely worth your time to see what a simple Internet search reveals.

CHAPTER 8

Board Interviews

As with any job, getting on a board requires an interview. If you are pursuing board service, you have likely been through your fair share of interviews. But a board interview is unique. This chapter covers how to leave a good first impression; what to expect at your board interview; how to prepare for a board interview; what to do before, during, and after the board interview; and what to look out for while interviewing. While you cannot control everything, by being prepared and knowing what to expect, you are more likely to join a board where you are a fit and that will be a rewarding professional experience.

How to Prepare for Board Interviews?

Your first impression can either make or break your chances of joining a board of your dreams. For a board position, making a first good impression is not something that can be achieved in one day or within few hours. This is not something that can happen as a fluke! It is a process with multiple stages. You need to prepare so that when the right time comes, you can make your move, shine, and ultimately get noticed.

- **Know and articulate your unique value proposition**
  Companies are looking for professionals who have industry insights, experience, or expertise in fields that will benefit their company. You must know and repeatedly articulate your unique value proposition in different ways. Which companies would benefit from your background? What special experience do you have? What doors can you open? What insights can you provide? Ultimately, what sets you apart and makes you a perfect fit for a specific board opportunity?

List your relevant experience, expertise, and achievements. Also, list roles where you have helped a company grow. You need to clearly and succinctly articulate your value proposition for the company, highlighting your experiences and expertise. If you can do this well, it will significantly increase your chances of being selected for the board.

- **Understand the company**

  As simple as this may sound, many people fall short of this requirement. You must understand a few key details about the board that you are being interviewed for. This can include the company's mission, vision, and cultural values. If the company has a website, you should visit it periodically before the interview to make sure you are up to date with important information. You could also visit the company's social media pages. Finally, try to do independent research on the company, its chief executive officer (CEO), founders, and executives both on the Internet and through your network. Understanding the company will most certainly give you an edge.

- **Staying current in your industry and field**

  Staying updated with the company's affairs and its industry is very important for directors. This will not only make you aware of what is happening at the company but can also help you make a good first impression as a prospective director.

- **Continue learning**

  Have an open mind and project an attitude of excitement about learning and collaboration. Be your own toughest critic and constantly evaluate where you are lacking in terms of skills, knowledge, and network. Join seminars, update your skills, and attend industry events and trade shows. Prioritize your learning and development and stay on top.

- **Know the expected dress code**

  This is very important and should never be taken for granted. Never assume you know what to wear to the interview—make sure you have a clear understanding of what is appropriate and expected. You need to fit into the culture of the company at the highest level from the day one; there may not be a second chance to get it right. The last thing that you want to do is show up for the interview like it is a cocktail party or golf tournament.

- **Understand your reason for being there**

  Have you ever showed up for an interview looking lost? Do you know how embarrassing this can be? Not only does this reduce your chance of being invited to join as a director, but it can also damage your self-esteem. To avoid this scenario, make sure you properly understand why you are being considered for this position, what the company needs, and how your background fits in.

What to Expect at a Board Interview?

At a minimum, the board interviews are usually conducted by the chairperson, the presiding or the lead director of the board, members of the nomination committee or the governance committee, and the CEO of the company. It is not unusual to also meet other directors, executives, and other company stakeholders such as investors, advisors, and key employees. The style, frequency, and length of the interview will vary greatly from company to company.

Consistently articulate your unique value proposition and qualifications throughout the interview process. Your experience, achievements, knowledge, expertise, interests, and connections will ultimately set you apart.

You will be asked different types of questions to ascertain your ability to constructively collaborate and bond with other directors, executives, stakeholders, vendors, partners, suppliers, and their network.

Questions to expect:

- Tell me about yourself.
- What are your personal objectives and goals?
- What value will you bring to the company? How?
- What strategies may you suggest for the company?
- What do you know about the company and its unique history, position in the marketplace, and vision?
- Why do you want to serve on this board?
- How much experience do you have as a board director?
- What are you currently doing professionally?
- What skills do you have to serve the board?
- What is a summary of your achievements and experience?
- What is your background?

- How do you handle complex situations in your professional life?
- How much time can you give to this organization?
- How do you deal with conflict?
- Do you have any questions for me?

What Kind of Questions Should You Ask?

You should be prepared to ask questions throughout your interview process. Here are a few of the questions that Nancy Sheppard instructs her clients to consider asking. Some questions are not as appropriate for your initial interviews but should be addressed as you progress in the process.

- As a board member, what if anything, keeps you up at night regarding the company?
- What are a few of the key strategic issues that the board has faced in the past year?
- What do you see as the biggest challenges facing the board?
- What are the strengths of this board? Where could it improve?
- What kind of board development program do you have? Are there any certification requirements for the directors?
- How does the board evaluate their own performance? What could be improved?
- How does the board evaluate the CEO's performance—on what basis?
- How does the board stay current on new and evolving technologies and their potential impact on the company's industry, strategy, and business model?
- What is the onboarding process for a new member?
- Are there any risks on the horizon that I should know about before joining the board? Legal? Reputation? Compliance? Management Issues? Financial?

What Are the Best Practices for a Director Interview?

Board interviews can sometimes be very tricky. If you are not careful enough, you could miss an amazing board opportunity. There are many expectations for your behavior during a board interview. The following are some good places to start:

- **Be confident**

  You want to show your interviewers that you have a vast knowledge about the company and are ready to contribute toward its development as soon as you join. One way to exude confidence is to consistently demonstrate your unique value proposition that you bring to the board and how it is a match considering the current board composition and company's direction. Make sure your body language, speech patterns, and behaviors project confidence as well. As minor as it sounds, fidgeting can limit your chances!

- **Provide direct answers**

  You do not have all day for an interview. You should always be as direct as possible when answering questions. Observe your answers as you provide them. When it looks like you are staring to digress, stop.

- **Respect your interviewers and their time**

  Take every possible opportunity to leave a good impression on your interviewers. The most effective way to do this is to give them the utmost respect. Your interviewers are constantly taking note of both your statements and behavior at every given point in time during the interview, so this can truly make a difference. Be respectful, stay gracious, listen well, comment thoughtfully, and behave appropriately. Even if you seem to have a rapport with the interviewers, do not get so relaxed that you crack excessive jokes or speak too casually or too much.

- **Perfect a positive verbal and nonverbal language**

  Make sure you maintain comfortable eye contact. Sit properly and maintain good posture. For example, avoid sitting as if you are in a bar or a restaurant. Convey a professional, poised demeanor. Conduct yourself appropriately, intentionally, and with integrity. Your goal is to demonstrate good judgment in every interaction and in every action. So be sure to pay attention to details.

- **Be forward and candid**

  Your answers must be accurate, credible, forward, complete, and honest. No board wants to hire someone who is not honest; being evasive does not project integrity. This requires you to be disciplined, think through your answers, and listen carefully. If it looks like you have made a mistake, correct it as soon as you can to avoid any suspicion or confusion and move forward. Practice doing this in a seamless, natural, and credible way.

- **Articulate your unique value proposition, background, experience, and expertise**

  Interviews often start with an exchange about your resume as well as your background. You will need to highlight information about past occupations or any board experiences which prepared you for this role. Other inquiries might be based on past associations and how your connections can influence the company's needs. Also expect questions about your ability to collaborate, understanding of the industry, understanding of the company, its history and its stakeholders, as well as your understanding of your role as a director.

- **Be clear about how your skills, expertise, experience, and traits are a good fit**

  Expect inquiries about your aptitudes and experience in issues such as finances, communications, advertising, or industry-related information. It is important to focus on high-level experiences and strategy in the relevant industry.

- **Leverage your connections and networking**

  Every director brings new connections to the board and the company. It is not unusual for companies to rely on their directors to open doors, maintain relationships, and be ambassadors. Expect questions about your network and how it can be leveraged to benefit the company.

- **Demonstrate passion and commitment**

  Passion and commitment to the company, industry, and stakeholders build a strong case for a solid board applicant. Why do you want to join the board of this specific company? What about its product or people excites you? Are you prepared to stick around long term through good and bad? Make sure you can genuinely articulate your passion and commitment to the role, company, and industry that you are interviewing for.

What to Avoid at the Board Interview?

Being successful in a board interview requires that you understand what is always expected of you. This means that there are dos and don'ts in this process that you must follow. What follows are some of the things that you should never do at any board interview.

- **Do not be arrogant**
  Although being confident is good, as it helps your audience sense that you have a good understanding of the subject matter, avoid overdoing it. It may come across as arrogance, which will irritate your interviewers. Do not speak about a subject unless you have been asked to. There are times when it will look like you have made a mistake. As such, you will want to get corrected by your interviewers. If this happens, do not interrupt their flow as your actions could be interpreted as arrogance and disrespect.

- **Do not be scared**
  This is another issue that can limit your chances of getting appointed. You need to avoid the temptation of expressing yourself in a way which shows that you fear your audience. Be in control of the situation by feeling relaxed about providing answers to questions which have been thrown at you. If you have trouble talking to a group of people, then you may need to start working on your speaking skills before attempting a board interview. Interviews will rarely be one-on-one.

- **Do not be sloppy**
  Even if you think you know the company's culture, do not make assumptions about what you should wear. You want to ensure that you understand what the dress code is for your interview. This can really help to ensure that you are not taking a shot in the dark. When in doubt, ask! It is better than showing up looking clueless.

- **Do not be distracted**
  Consider not focusing more on the benefits attached to the position than on the roles that you are expected to play. This can lead you to leave out little details which will help you get such an appointment. Try as much as you can not to get overexcited during the interview. Focus on consistently reiterating your value proposition.

- **Do not be clueless or underprepared**

  Ensure that you understand how you can contribute to the company as a director. Why did they choose to interview you? What value do you bring in their eyes? This requires researching the role and reviewing your unique fit.

What to Do after a Board Interview?

After your board interviews, you may not be sure what steps to take next. What follows are some ideas of what you can do after going through a board interview:

- **Analyze your performance**

  This is the right time to be honest with yourself about how you performed over the course of the interview. One of the ways to get this right is to recall your interviewers' reactions to your answers. Try to remember their body language and responses. It is a good idea to reflect about what you did well and what you can improve.

- **Be expectant**

  Have you just finished an interview where you think that you performed excellently? This is not the time to rest on your laurels and keep your fingers crossed. Rather, you should take the opportunity to start practicing the roles you would be expected to fulfill if you are appointed.

  Always check your mail and expect your phone to ring. This can show that you are optimistic about the board position. You can also ask your interviewers how they will follow up with you. If the interview went well, they will be glad to let you know.

- **Thank your interviewers**

  This could be the difference between you getting appointed and being turned down. You need to ensure that you have thanked your interviewers before leaving. This has nothing to do with whether you answered questions professionally. Saying thank-you shows that you are a true professional—someone they can trust with the highest degree of responsibility.

- **Stay calm**

  Over 50 percent of interviewers are usually interested in the ways people behave before, during, and after an interview. Most of them are not very interested in the questions they are asking—they are more interested in carefully observing your reactions and how you craft your answers. You must keep your cool, regardless of how you have answered the questions thrown at you. This is one period where you do not want to get too emotional. This can limit your chances of being appointed as a member of the board.

Conclusion

Congratulations! You have just taken a huge step in your board journey. By reading this book (and completing the worksheets in the appendixes) you have invested in your future as a director.

So, what now?

I tried my best to put as much information as possible in this book, but it is still essentially a beginner's guide. And, of course, everyone's board journey is unique, just as every person is unique. Appendix C has a list of organizations that can assist you in taking the next steps or share other resources.

If you have any further questions that you would like me to answer in future editions, you can get in touch with me on my website: http://olgamack.com/contact/. Please share your board-related documents, tips, templates, and examples to be used as examples and templates in future editions.

I wish you the best of luck on your journey to board service!

APPENDIX A

Board-Readiness Worksheets

These board-readiness worksheets can help guide you through the process of getting ready for board service.

The Roadmap to Target Your Unique Value Proposition and *Board Biography and Board Opportunities* worksheets will help you crystallize what you bring to boards and what boards may be interested in your skills. I am confident that you will find this worksheet helpful because Nancy Sheppard has tested it with numerous clients.

The Networking Plan can help you identify and categorize key people you should network with, as well as groups to connect with and events to attend.

The Board-Ready Thought Leader worksheet will help you plan for the three stages of board readiness: joining, shaping, and driving the conversation in your relevant industry.

Roadmap to Target Your Unique Value Proposition, Board Biography, and Board Opportunities

3–5 areas of expertise a board would value?	Why? What have you accomplished using this expertise? Provide metrics to show your success.
E.g., Growth strategy and leadership	E.g., Developed and presented growth strategy to the board of 7—doubling company's market cap from $12B to $25B via an acquisition, while managing a $140M budget.

Board profile and elevator pitch	A short paragraph that sums up your expertise.
	E.g., I am a C-Level financial services and fintech executive who leads strategic transformation and growth through rapid technology, regulatory and market changes.

What industries could value your expertise?	Why? What is your experience with these industries?
My skills are not industry specific *E.g., CFO for Audit*	

What are your personal goals?	Pick	What	Why or other comments
Why do you want to be on a board? E.g., *Improve My Network, Give Back, Financial Rewards, Board Service Career after "retirement."*	5–10 top reasons		
Personal "wish list" for your board service: E.g., *High Regard for Management, Strong Ethics Culture, Board Dynamics are Positive . . .*	5–10 most important		
Industries of most interest to you E.g., *B2B security software, hardware, and professional services . . .*	3–5		
What's your passion? E.g., *Interior Design, AI, Scaling*	2–3		
Specific companies that will address your value and passion. E.g., *Interior Design— Helping Houzz and monetize their services through AI, Big Data, and developing partnerships*	3–5		

What company strategic goals or life cycle stage best fit your goals and expertise?	Yes	No	Why?
Rapid growth (organic)			
Growth by acquisition			
Digital transformation			
Disruptor/innovator			
Global expansion			
Distressed/turnaround			

What type and size company best fit your goals and expertise?	Yes	No	Why?
Nonprofit board			
Advisory board			
Private—Closely held or family (small to mid)			
Private—Closely held or family (large)			
Private—Early stage startup			
Private—VC/PE backed (series B–D)			
Private—Late stage/ Pre-IPO			
Public—Micro/small cap			
Public—Mid cap			
Public—Large			
International HDQ private (note countries)			
International HDQ public (note countries)			
Specialty—i.e., mutual fund, REIT other			

Networking Plan

Create a spreadsheet or document to identify and track your contacts

Decision makers	
Chairpersons	Board members
VCs/PE Firms	CEOs
Connectors, mentors, and advocates	
Industry Leaders/Influencers (Lawyers, Accountants, Professionals)	Executives (CFOs, GCs, COOs)
Others	
Groups and organizations	Events and conferences

Become a Board-Ready Thought Leader

The following article was first published on the Association of Corporate Counsel (ACC) Docket (available at http://www.accdocket.com/articles/ raising-your-profile-to-get-board-ready.cfm). It explains the Become a Board-Ready Thought Leader worksheet that follows it.

SC Moatti has the soft smile and all-knowing gaze of a woman who has been there and done it all. We met at The Battery in San Francisco, where she meets with people twice a week to discuss topics of mutual interest—and she has many interests. After all, Moatti is a technology visionary, a VC investor, and the best-selling author of Mobilized: An Insider's Guide to the Business and Future of Connected Technology (Berrett-Koehler Publishers; May 2, 2016). She also serves on boards of directors for both public and private companies, including mobile technology giant Opera Software (OPERA, Oslo).

SC Moatti, who started her career as a product professional before becoming an executive at mobile pioneers like Facebook, Trulia, and Nokia, approached her board search pragmatically. She modeled her strategy on previous business development experiences. Moatti has launched and monetized mobile products that are now used by billions of people and have received prestigious awards, including an Emmy nomination. Likewise, she views herself as a product that needs to appeal to a certain market where perfect fit is of the essence: board appointment committees.

"Being board-ready is a new mindset and most people will need to reinvent and re-package themselves at least to some extent to become board-ready," says Moatti. "Reinventing ourselves as many as seventeen times or even more throughout our career is an essential professional skill to thrive in the ever-changing social, political, and technological landscape." She adds, "In fact, if a professional fails to do that, she will reach the middle career plateau within two to five years."

Moatti draws inspiration from John T. Chambers, executive chair and former CEO of Cisco Systems. Chambers, who led Cisco as CEO for 20 years, believes that every company must rethink and reinvent itself every 3 to 6 years. "It is only logical that people need to do the same to keep with the same changes," Moatti explains. "That's the only way to stay relevant in any business."

Her plan to transition from the C-suite to the boardroom was simple—become a board-ready thought leader in a field and then look for others who seek this leadership. So she proactively asked herself: "How do you go from being an industry expert to becoming a board-ready thought leader?" Moatti developed a surprisingly simple framework to increase her visibility and raise her profile for board opportunities. The framework consists of three steps that are continuously repeated and refined: join, shape, and drive.

Join the Conversation

"The first step is to join the conversation of a function or industry," Moatti explains. "This requires a little more than just doing your job well." She recommends doing some combination of the following: chairing or hosting events, hosting speakers, sharing curated content on social media, blogging, or speaking. "This will most certainly connect you with interesting people that you did not know before," says Moatti.

"When I started on this journey, I decided to curate news or tweet something every day, speak once a month, and write a blog entry once a month," shares Moatti. "I started very small." Of course, this required an effort on top of her already loaded professional schedule. "Every day I was looking for something good to retweet," she says. "And it is surprisingly hard to find high-quality writing that adds to the conversation in the sea of mediocre internet writing. Doing so forced me to read and stay current." Writing was also initially challenging for Moatti. "Writing relatively good, well-researched material takes time. And then there's validating, editing, and placing your work in a respectable publication. All of this requires an effort and is not simple," she explains.

The effort paid off, however, and launched Moatti as a key participant in her industry. Soon enough, she found herself on numerous tech panels and included in new conversations. According to Moatti, the opportunity for expedited learning is the greatest reward of going through this conversation-joining process. "It also improved my research skills, my ability to think critically, and my ability to stay current with the developments in my field and business in general," Moatti adds.

Shape the Conversation

After a while, Moatti was able to do a little more. She started actively commenting on articles written by industry leaders, moderating discussions, and expressing her opinions on Twitter. "It felt only natural to start actively participating in the conversation that I joined," she explains. "Why else would I join, if not to participate?"

Moatti recommends having content-based discussions in your industry or function and being more proactive in seeking interesting opportunities. "In addition to my existing goals, I actively reached out to event organizers to moderate panels. I also contacted blogs to publish my opinions," Moatti says. She developed her own perspectives and began eagerly sharing them on Twitter, instead of merely retweeting the thoughts of others. This helped her grow and gain prominence as an industry leader.

Drive the Conversation

Eventually, Moatti and her positions became well known in her industry. "I decided to become best in class in my line of business," she explains. "I realized that I have significant views about product development and that writing articles and opinion pieces didn't provide enough space to express the breadth and depth of my thoughts." Moatti realized that she was no longer satisfied with simply participating in the industry conversation. "I wanted to drive my discipline in a certain direction," she says. So when the opportunity to write a book arose, Moatti eagerly took it.

"Writing a book is a whole different endeavor," says Moatti. "It is complex, time-consuming, and difficult." Moatti wrote the manuscript over the summer and published it a year after she signed a contract with a publisher. "It was my summer project, and I loved it!" she says. "Putting words on paper in long form helped me to refine my thoughts, to take bolder and more substantiated stands."

Moatti also regularly leads keynote addresses at industry conferences. "Panels are largely reactive," Moatti explains. She adds, "When you give a keynote speech, the bar is much, much higher. You need to really capture the attention of your audience and meet its needs; it is a performance. You need to be funny, memorable, relevant, current, and entertaining."

Since joining the board of Opera Software a couple of years ago, there has not been a dull moment. The company just wrapped up a major strategic initiative culminating in the sale of a major division (half of the business) to a Chinese consortium. "The transaction required regulatory approval across three continents," says Moatti. "Becoming board-ready is only the beginning of another journey, it never ends!"

Although it has required great effort, Moatti has used the "join, shape, drive" framework to gain new skills, refine her perspectives, and successfully transform from an industry expert to a board-ready thought leader. By increasing her visibility as a valuable industry player, Moatti gained the credibility and opportunities needed to become board-ready. And although she has earned positions on boards for both public and private companies, Moatti refuses to rest on her laurels. Always reinventing herself, she is already focused on continuing the cycle. In 3 to 6 years, we can expect to see Moatti back at The Battery, discussing her latest visionary transformation.

Complete the Become a Board-Ready Thought Leader worksheet on the next page to create your "join, shape, drive" plan.

Stage	Your actions
Join the conversation	
Shape the conversation	
Drive the conversation	

APPENDIX B

Board Profile and Competency Matrix

A competency matrix gives a rundown of crucial competencies a board needs to do a good job. It can be utilized to understand and create your board profile and hone your unique value proposition. In other words, filling out the competency matrix can help you assess the value that you can bring to a board. This tool can also be used to assess the existing competencies of your target company's corporate board, which can help you understand where you fit in.

Board Profile and Competency Matrix

General director competency matrix	Self-assessment
Relevant professional experience	
Governance	
Business/management	
Legal/regulatory	
Human resources	
Accounting/financial	
Risk management	
Public relations/media	
Other	
Specialized knowledge	
Government/public policy	
Community/stakeholder relations	
Industry/sector	
Other	
Personal skills	
Leadership/teamwork	
Strategic thinking/planning	
Critical thinking/problem-solving	
Other	
Other	

APPENDIX C

Board Search Resources

The following table lists prominent organizations that can assist in your board-service journey. They range from advocacy groups to executive search services. While there is no substitute for personal research, education, and networking, these groups can provide further resources.

Board-Search Resources

Company	Website
2020 Women on Boards	https://www.2020wob.com/
Advancing Women Execs	http://inawe.com/
Ascend	http://www.ascendleadership.org/
Atlanta Women's Foundation (Atlanta)	https://atlantawomen.org/women-on-board/
Athena Alliance	https://athenaalliance.org/
Broadrooms	http://broadrooms.com/
Caldwell Partners	www.caldwellpartners.com
Catalyst	www.catalyst.org/corporate-board-services-allies
Chadick Ellig	http://chadickellig.com/expertise/
DirectWomen	www.directwomen.org
Directors Academy	http://directorsacademy.com/programs/
Directors & Boards	www.directorsandboards.com/
DiverseCity onBoard	http://diversecityonboard.ca/
Diverse Director DataSource (CalSTRS and CalPERS) through Equilar	www.calstrs.com/diverse-director-datasource
DiversifiedSearch	http://diversifiedsearch.com/
Egon Zehnder	www.egonzehnder.com/
Equilar Diversity Network	www.equilar.com/diversity
Executive Leadership Council (ELC)	www.elcinfo.com/

Company	Website
HACR	www.hacr.org/
Heidrick & Struggles	www.heidrick.com/
KPMG Board Leadership Center	https://boardleadership.kpmg.us/
Latino Corporate Directors Association	http://latinocorporatedirectors.org/
LEAP	www.leap.org/
MontaRosa	http://montarosa.com/
Nurole	www.nurole.com/
Onboard (Atlanta)	www.onboardnow.org
Private Company Director	www.privatecompanydirector.com
Savoy	http://savoynetwork.com/category/business/power-300-most-influential-black-corporate-directors/
Silicon Valley Directors Exchange (SVDX)	www.svdx.org
SpencerStuart	www.spencerstuart.com/
Stanford Women on Boards	www.gsb.stanford.edu/alumni/communities/womens-programs/stanford-women-boards-initiative
theBoardlist	https://theboardlist.com
Thirty Percent Coalition	www.30percentcoalition.org/
Topmark Advisors	http://topmarkadvisors.com/
Trewstar	www.trewstar.com/
United States 30% Club	https://30percentclub.org/
Women2Boards	https://women2boards.com/
Women Corporate Directors (WCD) Foundation	www.womencorporatedirectors.org/
Women in the Boardroom	http://womenintheboardroom.com
Women Serve on Boards	www.womenserveonboards.com

APPENDIX D

Examples of Board Profile (aka Unique Value Proposition, "Super Power," or Elevator Pitch)

The following are illustrative examples of board profiles (aka unique value proposition, "super power," or elevator pitch). When crafting your biographies, it can be helpful to read board biographies from your target board opportunities. These can be found or deduced from company websites or director LinkedIn profiles. These model board pitches can help you to craft your own unique value proposition. Please note that all company names and contact information have been anonymized. Some information has been redacted in brackets to preserve anonymity.

Jill is C-level financial services and fintech executive and advisor who leads strategic transformation in the face of rapid technology, regulatory, and market changes. Brings a blend of consulting and corporate executive experience for industry leaders including Bain, PayForward, and Master-Card. Utilizes 25 years of experience repositioning and scaling companies through innovation, new product, market, talent, capability development, and M&A. She is well positioned to add value in the boardroom of a company in the payment processing space.

Guy is a successful C-Level corporate executive, founder, CEO, and director. An entrepreneur with over 20 years of experience in manufacturing, he focuses on helping companies and individuals thrive during transitions. Leaning from his experiences building a highly engaged board of directors at the companies he founded, Guy has served on numerous corporate boards in the manufacturing, technology, and service industries.

Jared is an experienced public company director with extensive finance and operations experience. A former CFO for three technology companies through significant IPO, growth, and M&A. He has served as an advisor for high numerous startups and as a director and audit committee chair. He is known for his skills in strategy and managing profitability. He would be of tremendous value to a high growth company. Jared has a broad stakeholder point of view from his work as the CFO, an advisor, and a board chair.

Nancy is C-level executive and advisor with expertise in mobile, consumer products, and connectivity that form the backbone of today's IoT. Her strengths in developing strategy, launching and running fast growth, innovative e-commerce businesses grew from her leadership in scaling two consumer online businesses to $500M during her 20 years with Well-Known Company A and Well-Known Company B. Her experience on a board of a startup private company acquired by Company C adds to her overall knowledge of bringing significant value to founders and investors.

Fintech Thought Leader, Strategy Executive, Product Executive, and Process Innovation Executive

Francis is a C-level financial services and fintech executive and advisor who leads strategic transformation in the face of rapid technology, regulatory, and market changes. Brings a blend of consulting and corporate executive experience for industry leaders including PayForward, and HappyTime, with unique perspective on what it takes for Executive Teams and Board of Directors to define ambitious, yet achievable visions and pursue organic and inorganic growth. Utilizes 25 years of experience repositioning and scaling companies through innovation, new product, market, talent, capability development, and M&A. Anticipates and identifies relevant trends, develops tangible responses and guides companies through high stake changes—from aligning product portfolios and organizations to identifying M&A targets and integrating newly acquired companies.

Driving Business Strategies through Disruptive Technologies and Investor Insights

Sue Dollar is a SEC qualified financial and blockchain expert whose research experience in finance, investments and disruptive technologies provides companies insights on competing in a rapidly changing world. As an institutional investor, financial expert and fintech advisor, she is well versed in strategizing about business use cases for enterprise and public blockchain, cryptocurrencies, and token economics. Sue's experience includes working for investment firms representing diverse strategies such as emerging and aggressive growth, long/short hedge, GARP, and value. In addition, she has extensive experience evaluating funding sources. Her career experience provides boards a valuable understanding of innovations that impact how a company's products and processes will care with the competition going forward.

Jane is a marketing industry veteran and award-winning influencer with a wealth of experience in growing and transforming consumer brands. She focuses on companies in production, hospitality, or retail. She is experienced in defining marketing strategy and leading brand growth or transformation in over three decades for iconic brands with Company A, Company B, and Company C. In her most recent 5-year CMO position at Company C, her team doubled profitability while increasing sales by 125 percent.

With extensive executive and board experience in risk, strategy, cybersecurity, data, digital marketing, and analytics, Kate is looking to join the board of an innovative company adding new products or services. She wants to assist their digital strategy positions for greater top-line growth and favorable brand position.

Lee is a qualified financial expert with experience as an Audit partner of BBBB and as CFO of a $100 million company which acquired three private companies in his tenure. He is looking to join a corporate board of a small private family company where his expertise in expansion, M&A, and succession planning with family-owned businesses would be valued. He focuses on companies in production, hospitality, or services.

Olga is a seasoned director and chief strategy officer with a successful track record of combining leadership, innovation and financial expertise to guide enterprise-wide initiatives. She is highly regarded for her ability to provide strategic and operational insights. Olga is an innovator and recognized industry thought leader, she consistently anticipates needs and creates solutions ahead of the curve. Her experiences include startup, rapid growth, mature, consolidation, regulated, and traditional businesses.

Natalie's leadership roles in manufacturing, global operations, strategy, finance, and transformation a company would also be an asset to a company eager to expand their footprint globally or assist a distressed company in turnaround strategy. Her 30 years of experience span a diverse set of company environments including startup, rapid growth, mature, consolidation, regulated, and traditional businesses ranging in size from $300 million to $10 billion in revenue.

Companies in transition, working to scale for growth and/or pre- or post-IPO would benefit from Peter's expertise in developing high-performance teams. He has built strong relationships with the investment community, both equity and debt. He has significant capital markets, restructuring, M&A, and divestitures experience.

Debbie is an investor relations executive with over 40 years of experience in private equity, investment banking and asset management. She has raised over $20 billion in capital for private investment funds over the course of her career with firms such as Iconic Company A Iconic Company B, Iconic Company C, Iconic Company D, and Iconic Company E. Her experiences span a across diverse industries including technology, services, and manufacturing. She also acquired expertise in services and medical devices corporate development through direct investment. Her experience makes her a good addition to boards that desire a director to add capital markets knowledge.

A company going through a major transformation, IPO, or M&A is where Beth thrives. She has a strong track record in driving profitable growth and has held leadership and P&L responsibilities. Her experiences span a across diverse industries including technology, services, and manufacturing.

Mona is a seasoned executive with more than 25 years advising Fortune 500 C-Suite executive, compensation, and audit committees. She has a unique combination of extensive experiences, including IPO, M&A, international expansion, risk management, deep regulatory understanding, and P&L responsibility.

APPENDIX E

Examples of Board Biographies and Board Resumes/CVs

The following are illustrative examples of board resumes and board biographies. When crafting your biography, it can be helpful to read board biographies from your target companies offering board opportunities. These can be found on company websites or sometimes on director LinkedIn profiles. These model board biographies and resumes/CVs can help you to craft your own unique board documents. Please note that all company names and contact information have been anonymized (unless specifically requested otherwise). Some information has been redacted in brackets to preserve anonymity.

Please note that much of the formatting of the original board biographies (usually the one-page requirement) and board resumes/CVs (which are limited to two or a maximum of three pages) has been lost in preparation publishing this book. I had to balance readability and substance while formatting and ultimately chose substance.

This appendix also includes recommendations about word choice for board biographies and board resumes/CVs to help you to stand out and get closer to achieving your board goals.

Board Biography Samples

Sue Dollar, CFA, MBA

*Driving Business Strategies through Disruptive Technologies and Investor Insights.
SEC Financial Expert and Blockchain Expertise.*

222 Main Street, San Francisco • (415) XXX-XXXX • LinkedIn • Sue@gmail.com

Sue Dollar's research experience in finance, investments, and disruptive technologies provides companies insights on competing in a rapidly changing world. As an institutional investor, financial expert, and fintech advisor, she is versed in strategizing about business use cases for enterprise and public blockchains, cryptocurrencies, token models, and more broadly, token economics. Sue's buy-side experience includes working for investment firms representing diverse strategies such as emerging growth, aggressive growth, long/short hedge, GARP, and value, and she has extensive experience evaluating funding sources.

Sue's domain expertise includes multiple technology industries, M&A and audit analysis, financial statements, and SEC filings. She qualifies as an audit committee-designated SEC financial expert and has extensive knowledge of corporate governance issues (nom/gov committee), vote on Say on Pay decisions and understands compensation structures most appealing to institutional investors (compensation committee). She brings companies an understanding of investors' preferred business models, messaging for long-term valuation premium as well as experience with proxy votes, ISS, trading liquidity issues, and M&A messaging.

Her cutting-edge research background provides her a platform to advise companies on the value of emerging technologies to transform their business. She analyzes why, or if, blockchain is important to a business and assists them in navigating their strategy as an enterprise software company relative to risks and business opportunities with this new revolutionary technology. She conceptualizes opportunities and risks around M&A targets generally, and specifically as it pertains to the changing architecture of enterprise software.

Sue leads technology research at Bigtime Investment Partners, a large advisory firm with $8B+ in assets under management, where she evaluates strategies, positioning, financials, and valuation of technology companies. Sue evaluates a wide range of industries including analytics, hybrid cloud, public and private blockchain, open source, IoT, security, machine learning, AI, SaaS, smart cities, transportation automation, and many others. Additionally, she serves as an Advisor to Littletime Fintech, a company and social enterprise facilitating cash-to-virtual currency conversion through blockchain technology. Sue advises on strategy, potential synergistic technologies, partnerships, and on emerging funding models while preserving long-term options.

Previously, Sue served as the senior vice president of OXY Funds, a leading global asset management firm. In this role, she provided technology research for the $32B in large-cap growth managers' funds and convertibles bond funds. Sue comanaged OXY's Emerging Tech Funds. Previously, she comanaged the Global Technology Fund for BigtIme Funds, which returned 630% in its first 12 months and 499% and 425% in the succeeding 2 years, ranking it first by Lipper of all diversified mutual funds globally for 3 years. Sue was also the Technology Analyst for the Asia Pacific and Japan region. Sue started her investment career at Bakers Insurance.

Sue earned her MBA with an emphasis in finance from the University of Southern California and a BA in Economics from the University of California. Forbes presented her with the Award for Women in Fintech Research in 2015. Sue has served for the last 6 years on the Economics Leadership Council at UC. She coauthored strategic plans and annual reports for several local charities. Sue was a member of the 1986 Junior Olympics US gold medal team in soccer and placed ninth in the 2005 US World Cup League Finals. She runs ultramarathons throughout the world.

Juanita Pérez

123 Beautiful Street, Everytown, CA 91234 • jperez2000@hotmail.com

• 524-555-5555 (cell)

Juanita Pérez recently served as president/CEO of a $XXXm international manufacturing company and has served on boards and committees of privately held companies and nonprofit organizations. She is a certified SEC financial expert with an Elite University MBA. Juanita rose through successive leadership roles in global companies with functional expertise in finance, strategy, marketing, and product development. Juanita currently serves on boards and additionally specializes in executive coaching, interim CEO roles, and strategic consulting.

Since 1989, Juanita has served on fourteen boards for both private and not-for-profit organizations. Her first role as an independent director was with Family Co, a $Xb family-owned manufacturer of industrial equipment. She also served as a director of Everytown Incubator, an incubator for technology startups; Moneybanks Equity International, a $XXm private equity portfolio company; and Consumer Product Co, a division of Consumer Goods Company. In her role as president/CEO, Juanita managed multiple boards of distinct business units.

Juanita is currently an independent director on the boards of Family Matters, Inc., a family-owned distribution and fabrication company and Amazing Products, Inc., a components manufacturer, as well as serving as an advisor for Strategic Consultants Co, a strategy consulting firm for entrepreneurs. Juanita is a past board chair and CEO of NatureLearn, a nonprofit dedicated to STEM education based on nature literacy.

Most recently, Ms. Pérez was president and CEO of Dundermiff, a $XXXm division of Dundermiff Inc, a global technology company, manufacturing [products]. As president and CEO, Juanita was responsible for six business units with ten manufacturing locations, six sales offices, an R&D facility and corporate offices. Prior to Dundermiff, Ms. Pérez served as the VP/GM for Global Marketing and Product Management of Schrute Co., a $X billion division of BEET.

Prior to joining Schrute Co, Juanita Pérez spent 2 years with Halpert Industries where she was specifically recruited to the leadership team to help prepare the company for private equity sale or IPO.

When Juanita and her husband, Jim, purchased Printing Co, LLC, she utilized her ability to understand consumer behavior to turn around an unprofitable operation. As a business owner, she recognized the changing consumer demand for [service] and transformed the existing business model from [analog] to digital. Ms. Pérez has also held executive level positions with well-regarded brands such as X, Y, and the Z Company.

Ms. Pérez's career began as an International Economist with the U.S. Treasury Department. She earned an MBA from the Business School at the Elite University. She holds a masters in international relations from the Ultimate University School of International Relations and a bachelor's degree from Supreme University.

Juanita has also been a member of Secret Success Org, an invitation-only membership organization of the world's most successful women business leaders.

Jane Wong

Silicon Valley, CA 650-555-5555 • jwong@supremealumni.org • LinkedIn: JWong555

Enterprise Cloud Services Expert with Tech Product GM Leadership

Jane is the CEO of XYZ Software, an enterprise software company that is revolutionizing how businesses run in the cloud. XYZ's [technology]-based software platform dynamically optimizes and automates cloud services based on the most critical business objectives. Jane has rapidly grown enterprise software and consumer Internet businesses on the scale of $25M to $3.5B in annual revenue. She was formerly vice president and general manager of Software at LMNOP, where she created a new business and platform for offering enterprise software solutions—DevOps, Cybersecurity, Big Data, and App Development—to SMB, Mid-Market, and Large Enterprise customers. Jane had strategy, P&L, and operational responsibilities, and she was focused on engaging customers and partners through several new digital experiences, digital marketing, and specialized sales models to drive growth in net new customers and revenue.

Prior to LMNOP, Jane held 6 years of product leadership roles at Yahoo! Most notably, Jane was senior director of product management for Hello Search & E-Commerce (Hello Shopping, Travel, Autos, and Homes), where she launched consumer Internet innovations that drove X00 million daily visits and $X.5 billion in revenue. Jane was also responsible for several initiatives to deliver new consumer experiences, improve monetization in digital advertising, increase Search market share, and promote product selection and sales through partnerships.

Prior to joining Hello in 2007, Jane spent 3 years at ZIA Global Services as a senior consultant in the supply chain and customer relationship management practices focused on providing supply chain, order management, customer service, and channel marketing solutions to clients in the high-tech, medical device, travel insurance, and retail industries.

Jane is a director of Food Co (NASDAQ: []) and Education Inc (NYSE: [ ]). She serves on the audit and nominating and governance committees for Food Co, and she is the chair of the business advisory committee for Education Inc and serves on its compensation committee. She is also an advisory director of Advertising Tech, a late-stage VC-backed tech company based in San Francisco. She has been recognized in The Prominent Diversity Association's Top 50 Most Powerful Women in Technology and Tech Industry Business Journal's 40 Under 40.

Jane received a BS in computer science and an MS in management science and engineering, both from Supreme University. She speaks Mandarin Chinese conversationally and plays USVA 4.5 adult league volleyball.

Sofia Syed

sofiasyed@scientificinvestment.com • 415-555-5555 • LinkedIn: XXX, Sesame, A

Sofia Syed is the managing director of Scientific Investment Company, LLC, a 38-year-old investment and advisory firm. Ms. Syed is a biotechnology industry leader and a successful visionary thinker with more than 40 years of business experience in the life sciences industry and in venture capital investments. She is known for her wisdom and unifying abilities in her board-of-director work with multiple companies and startup venture enterprises. Her international experience and her grasp of the business of science is a unique perspective. She brings value to the classroom as an adjunct professor at the University of Gotham in the Department of Analytics and Technology in the School of Management.

Currently, Ms. Syed serves on the board of directors of BioTech Leading Co. She serves on the audit committee, nominating and governance committee, and is the chair of the compensation committee. She is a director of BioSciences Leaders Inc. She is a director of Medical Startup in Metropolis. She serves on the board of advisors to Female Entrepreneurs Org, a nonprofit organization dedicated to advancing women entrepreneurs. She also serves as the chair of the American [Disease] Association Leadership Board for Silicon Valley. She is a graduate of the Supreme Law School Board of Directors College course, and a member of the Corporate Directors Group, which provides continuing education for directors.

From 2000 to 2005, she was a venture partner with MGS Capital GmbH, one of the first and largest venture capital firms in Germany. She sourced and invested in three companies and built out their San Francisco office while participating in the raising of their fifth fund of X31 million Euros.

She was a cofounder and the CEO of DNA, Inc., a [biotech] company, and wrote the first business plans for [project], as a consultant to Consultant Firm, and for [project], with Dr. Jane Doe, the founder. She was the first biotech analyst on Wall Street for Financial Firm and Banking Giant. She was the creator of two important conferences, The BioTech Conference in Metropolis and The Bio-Pharma-Conference in Europe. She and Katherine Doe started the publication, [title], which became the first online newsletter about biotechnology.

In 2003, she was included in [cultural organization] magazine's annual "Business 100" and received the Alumni Achievement Award from Mega College at Giant University in 2004. Ms. Syed is an avid horseback rider and mother of a daughter and a stepdaughter.

Erika M. Cramer*

Delivering board value through M&A, strategic leadership, asset management and corporate governance

San Francisco • New York • (914) 261.7775 • erika@canycap.com
• www.linkedin.com/in/erika-cramer-2034298/

Erika Cramer is an accomplished investment banking executive, advisor, and board member who leads corporate objectives and turnarounds resulting in billion-dollar outcomes through 25+ years in M&A, recapitalizations, capital raising, divestitures, succession planning, and valuations. She has strong expertise in corporate development and building entrepreneurial businesses that achieve strategic growth initiatives, enhance competitive positioning with risk controls, and enhance shareholder value. Erika is the architect of compliance and risk management protocols, establishing policies, procedures, and controls within highly regulated industries. She is highly qualified to serve on a board seeking strategic leadership, compliance oversight, asset management, and M&A acumen.

While serving as a partner and the chief compliance officer at Silver Lane Advisors LLC, Erika completed fifty-two transactions involving over $240B in assets under advisement/management (AUM) exchanging hands. Primarily focusing on small- to mid-sized transaction activity, she helped Silver Lane earn the reputation as the "go-to investment bank for wealth management M&A." Erika achieved trendsetting transactions—particularly in the niche areas of wealth management and fintech. She also developed all written policies and procedures for purposes of FINRA and the SEC, while developing new business and opening a branch in San Francisco.

Raising capital for investment products and early-stage companies is also within Erika's skillset and aligned with her expansive network. As a partner with Alternative Access Capital, Erika raised institutional capital for alternative investment products. At Silver Lane, she also raised several early-stage rounds of capital for fintech firms, even from organizations outside the traditional venture capital network.

Erika is currently a board director and the audit chair of the privately held Atlanta Life Financial Group and its subsidiary Atlanta Life Insurance Company. During her tenure she has led the board through a turnaround of the group life reinsurance and P&C businesses, while winding down an asset management firm that, at its peak, managed $10B in assets. She recruited an entirely new executive leadership team and non-statutory advisory board, along with establishing strategic client–vendor partnerships. Her work continues with implementation of its business plan and the company's overall transformation.

Erika is also a partner with CANY Capital, LLC, the sister firm of Alternative Access Capital, LLC, a private placement firm specializing in raising capital and hedge funds. She advises on wealth management strategies, reporting systems, and establishing multigenerational governance tools for the personal family practice of board directorships by sourcing and analyzing investment opportunities as well as selection and monitoring of external wealth managers and advisors.

Previously, Erika served as SVP, Strategic Development, for U.S. Trust Company of NY (formerly a subsidiary of Charles Schwab Corp.), and as a director and partner with Berkshire Capital Securities, LLC. A highly regarded speaker, Erika has organized, moderated, led, and designed many M&A and financial services-focused panel discussions. She conducted a TED-style talk for the CFA Society and has presented at industry-related conferences.

Erika is a board director of Trips for Kids Marin, which provides cycling experiences for underserved youth, where she has been involved with management/budget oversight, donor engagement, and recruitment of executive directors. She is a committee member and Angel for the Northern California Chapter of 100 Women in Finance where she has organized sponsored educational events. She is also a member of the National Association of Corporate Directors.

Erika earned an MBA in finance at Pace University and a bachelor's degree in finance from West Virginia University. She is licensed for Series 79, 7, 63, and 24, and earned an NAIC certificate for Statutory Accounting Principles. She is a triathlete, marathoner, and avid cyclist—a wife and mother to two daughters.

---

* *Erika M. Cramer's board biography has not been deidentified.*

Karla B. Great, MBA

Beautiful City, NY • 123-456-7890 • Karla@KarlaGreat.com • LinkedIn
Drives Growth with Capital Strategy and Investment Leadership Expertise

A board director and an investment executive, Karla B. Great, built a career helping company leaders maximize shareholder and stakeholder value—and has personally delivered half-a-billion dollars in revenue. As a consultative thought partner, growth driver, and management executive, she brings a unique blend of strategy, sales planning, and team development to her work scaling and building businesses.

Karla began her career at Iconic Bank A, before moving to Company A, where she played a pioneering role in the creation of a secondary market in capital equipment leases and portfolios. She then transitioned to Wall Street, working on the bond desk at iconic Bank B and later moving into investment management with Company B and subsequently iconic Company C. Prior to retiring from the investment field, Karla spent 11 years at the $##T privately held investment firm, Successful Investment Firm, where she led the public fund team and managed her own client base representing $###B+ in combined assets.

She holds an MBA in finance and economics from XXXXX School of Management and a BA in political science from XXXXXX University and is a 20XX Fellow of XXXXX University's XXXX Institute. Karla has completed board-readiness training. Her private and nonprofit board service includes governance, audit, finance, and investment committee leadership for institutions ranging from a startup investment fund to a $##B endowment. Current appointments include XXXXX Fund, XXXXXX University, XXXXXX Foundation, and XXXXX Foundation.

Karla was recognized in 20XX with The Women's XXXXXXXXXXXXXd's *Aiming High Award* and in 20XX with The Foundation for Beautiful City Public Schools' *Wall of Fame Humanitarian Award*. Speaking appearances include XXXXX University convocation, and Groundbreakers: Women in Leadership Summit, where she shared the stage with Gloria Steinem and Ali Wentworth. She coteaches design thinking at XXXXX University. Karla is currently writing stories about her life and has discovered a hidden talent: improv!

Amy S. Executive

Enabling Growth through Financial and Investment Management,
Risk Mitigation, and Financial Regulatory Expertise

Beautiful City, WA • amyexecutive@gmail.com
• (123) 456-7890 www.linkedin.com/in/amyexecutive

Amy is an accomplished global business executive and advisor with more than 30 years of experience in investment management operations, infrastructure development, finance, and global expansion. She is a financial expert and experienced audit committee member who delivers relevant, actionable information to boards and management on planning for, and mitigating, risk through strong business, financial and investment leadership, and deep financial regulatory expertise.

As a partner and the chief operating officer of XXXXXXX Advisors LP, Amy was instrumental in structuring and managing the growth from its inception as a $###M alternative investment advisor to an institutional, international investment advisory firm managing peak assets of $##B in several global hedge fund strategies. She supported the firm's SEC registration and registration with various global regulators. In collaboration with the firm's cofounders, Amy shaped business strategies, identified and implemented new initiatives, and played a key role in defining the firm's long-term trajectory and identity, while managing an $80M operating budget.

Amy is an industry pioneer and skilled negotiator who structured a unique package of counterparty agreements to mitigate credit, operations, and liquidity risks, providing XXXX guaranteed term financing. She oversaw the investment and custody of $XB in liquidity pool assets—allowing the firm to maintain its margin balances during the severe 20XX to 20XX market dislocation and to fund investor redemptions of $XB. Additionally, she served as an executive director, a financial expert, and an audit committee member of the board for several offshore hedge fund companies domiciled in the Cayman Islands and Luxembourg. Amy also led Taconic's counterparty risk function, where she introduced highly successful methods of mitigating counterparty custody risk—resulting in Taconic not incurring material counterparty losses during the 20XX Lehman collapse.

Previously, Amy served as the chief financial officer of XXXXXXX LLC. She was instrumental in forming a $XXM private equity fund investing in Eastern Europe, as well as developing the associated operations for the offices in both the United States and the EU. She structured various investment vehicles, including partnerships, limited liability companies, and offshore corporations. Prior to that role, Amy led as the corporate controller and assistant secretary for Great Company, Inc., where she managed the accounting department of the publicly traded software developer. She collaborated with the CFO, external accountants, and legal counsel on preparing and executing the company's IPO and Regulation S secondary offering. Amy played a key role in the company's subsequent pooling of interests' business combination and sale of non-core divisions in addition to directing the bank and cash management functions, coordinating audits and tax return preparation, and administering the stock option pool.

Amy is a member and managing director of Investment Circle, a network of angel investors dedicated to investing in early-stage companies that are founded and/or led by women. She is also a member of the Angel Group Association and an early-stage venture investor. Amy is a certified director in corporate governance, which she completed at a well-known university's school of management's executive education program. She also completed the comprehensive women's director development program at another well-known university's school of management. She was an accounting major at the University of XXXXXXX.

Robin Star, Esq., CPA
COO and CFO

XXXXXXXXXX, Inc.

INDUSTRIES

Technology, Design, Real Estate, Media and Entertainment, Biotech and Life Sciences

BOARD EXPERIENCES

- *Board Advisor,* XXXXXXXXXX
- *Treasurer,* XXXXXXXXXX
- *Secretary,* XXXXXXXXXX PUBLIC SCHOOLS
- *Secretary, Board Member,* XXXXXXXXXX ASSOCIATION XXXXXXXXXX SECTION
- *Member, Grant Committee,* XXXXXXXXXX FOUNDATION
- *Chairperson, Board of Advisors,* XXXXXXXXXX, INC.
- *Board Member, Audit Committee,* XXXXXXXXXX COLLEGE FOUNDATION
- *Secretary, Board Member, Finance, Governance, Integrations, and Audit Committees* XXXXXXXXXX Nonprofit

Known as a business innovator, Robin Star leads teams to success in operations, processes, and company culture. With over ## years of experience as a business executive in both public and private companies, Robin's career path has been about adapting to the moment, building versatility across all elements of a company, and providing cross-functional value. She uses her tenacity and natural inquisitive nature to spark action in teams to deliver superior results. Her extensive operations experience includes overseeing finance, human resources, information technology, sales operations, legal, procurement, and business processes. Robin is both an attorney and CPA who is passionate about people and building companies and teams.

Robin is the COO and CFO of XXXXXXXXXX, a privately held leading design, planning, and commercial reseller with over XXX employees with X locations in the United States. Selected as one of the Top 100 Fastest Growing Private Companies for 6 years in a row by the XXXXXXXXXX Business Times, XXXXXXXXXX is experiencing expansive growth. Robin heads all business operations and is charged with leading the company through its next phase with goals of doubling revenues and workforce.

Prior to XXXXXXXXXX, Robin was VP of Finance at XXXXXXXXXX (NASDAQ: XXXX) where she led business operations for the Beautiful City market. XXXXXXXXXX is the second largest media company in the United States with over XXX stations in XX markets. Robin was also the COO of XXXXXXXXXX University, an affiliate of XXXXXXXXXX Schools.

Robin started her legal and finance career as a senior manager with Big Four's National Tax office. She then went on to practice law as a corporate tax and employment lawyer at top law firms: National Law Firm A and National Law Firm B. Robin next transitioned to the corporate world where she worked as a senior attorney with XXXXXXXXXX (NASDAQ: XXXX) in its corporate headquarters in Beautiful City, TN and as an expat in Beautiful City, Germany. She was also counsel for the XXXXXXXXXX Foundation.

Robin then took a general management and human resources role becoming the executive director of the XXXXXXXXXX Organization where she led the organization's expansion to a premier national performing arts company. She later became the CFO of XXXXXXXXXX Media, a full-service multimedia company producing films, TV shows, and webisodes. Robin also produced an award-winning documentary on autism called XXXXXXXXXX, winner of the best short documentary at the 20XX American Pavilion in Cannes.

She has a passion for board service, with a focus on audit, finance, and governance issues. She earned her BS in accounting from the University of XXXXXXXXXX School of Commerce and her JD from the University of XXXXXXXXXX School of Law.

Board Resume/CV Samples

Sarah CV. Sample, CPA, MBA
SEC Financial Expert with Capital Markets and Fintech Leadership Expertise

Sarah Sample is a recognized SEC financial expert, senior executive, board director, and investor in the XYZ industry. She built and led HER Capital to over $500M in investments, and founded and grew Best Bank & Corporation's Investments Division, which became the most profitable division of the bank. Sarah's audit committee board service includes two corporate boards in the fintech and mobile marketplace. Her experience advising more than fifty public and private companies on complex financial transactions will be especially valuable for boardroom discussions at companies growing through acquisitions, with strategies to scale with that growth. Sarah maintains a global network of people at top XYZ industry companies built over several decades in investment banking and venture capital.

Key Areas of Expertise for Board Service

Leadership	Financial Experience/Skills	Industry Knowledge and Networking
Audit Committee	Complex Transactions	Financial
Chair	Private Equity Investing	Mobile Marketplace
Growth Plans	M&A	Emerging Technology
Business Strategy	IPOs	Private Equity
Customer Insights	Capital Markets	Venture Capital
Change Management		Global Market Connections
CEO Selection		

Board Experience

Fiduciary Boards
OneCompany (OTC: OCOM) *2012–present:* Provider of One Things in the ATM marketplace. *Annual revenue:* $225M. member of audit, compensation, and governance committees. Key role: Provided advice to management and the board regarding initial public offering.
GoshMobile (Privately held VC) *2010–present:* First company to offer customers option to get their daily Gosh via mobile delivery. *Annual revenue:* $50M. *Key roles:* Audit chair, responsible for introducing sales team to key mobile venture capitalists, and global connections to companies interested in partnering.
Advisory Boards
CLoudStore, (NASDAQ: SSSS) *2014–2016:* Technology company providing cloud storage of vital financial information. *Key role:* Strategic advisory board member for evaluation of merger opportunities, which resulted in purchase via BigStems (NASDAQ: XXXX) and return to shareholders of 544% return over 10 years.
Insure Me (Privately held VC) *2013–2014:* Online insurance app. *Key role:* Joined advisory board to assist in strategic and tactical plans for second round of funding which resulted in meeting goal of $250M for launch of second phase of app.
Non-Profit Boards and Trustee Positions
ABC Charity, *2010–present:* Board chair 2013–2015; Member of audit and executive committees. *Key roles:* Active board member for capital campaign for construction of new headquarters. Chaired the search committee in 2013 to bring in new CEO following strategic decision of board to expand the mission of the organization. Spearheaded rewrite of bylaws.
University of Someplace, *2008–2013:* endowment trustee. *Key Roles:* Trusted counselor regarding selection of a new investment management firm. Led the capital campaign for new sports stadium in 2010.
Public Television, *2001–2010:* audit chair 2006–2010 and finance committee. *Key roles:* Advisor for CEO and CFO during M&A analysis and multiyear budgeting processes and for selection of new auditors. Oversaw audit by PCBS regarding use of public funds.

HER Capital, Cofounder and General Partner (2001–Present)

- Cofounded HER Capital to assist smaller public and private companies prosper. As a senior partner, managed the firm's growth to over $500M by investing in 52 companies across five investment funds and a Global Partner Network. Today, the firm looks to her as the principal advisor regarding the capital markets environment and investments.

Best Bank & Corporation, SVP and Managing Director–Investments Division (1989–2001)

- Senior vice president and managing director of the Investments Division, a group that she founded in 1992. Her team advised retail financial institutions, consumer insurance companies, and retail firms on hundreds of mergers and equity capital markets transactions, including numerous IPOs. The division was the most profitable division of the bank from 1995 to 2001.
- As vice president, corporate development group (1989–1992), she was a founder of crazy but profitable ventures providing a significant source of increasing income for the bank.

Education

Master of Business Administration, MyBest Business School, Boston
Bachelor of Science in Finance and Accounting, University of California, Berkeley
Certified Public Accountant
Ongoing **director educational programs** through NACD workshops and conferences.

Speaking and Publications

Sarah speaks frequently on topics related to XYZ industry at conferences, workshops, private events, and webinars. She writes for numerous publications and is featured in news stories regularly. Here is a partial list from the last few years:

> **Technology and Investments**, Big Time Conference, Chicago, Feb. 2018
> **Mobile in the Marketplace** for X, A Global Event, London, Nov. 2017
> **How to Invest $2 Billion in Six Easy Steps**, Webinar, 2014
> **Sarah Sample: A Unique Woman in the Investment World**, New York Times, November, 2014

Recognition and Awards

Sarah has received numerous awards for her professional and nonprofit board work. Here are a few of the most recent and most relevant:

> **Most Outstanding Investor Advisors Nationwide**, New York Times, Nov. 2018
> **Leaders Who Matter**, Seattle Chronicle, June, 2017
> **Top 10 Women of the Year**, West Coast Investment Advisors, WCIA Conference, October 2016
> **Most Influential Women in Seattle**, Seattle Times, 2006–2010

Emeritus each year following 2010

Here is what a peer board member recently wrote about her:

> *"Sarah is a dedicated board member. She does her homework, presents her views diplomatically and is open to a full discussion of differences of opinion on the route our board should direct management to take. After serving on the audit committee with her for three years, I am confident that we are fulfilling our obligations, and that helps me sleep at night."*
>
> John A. Doe, CEO, LIittleBigMan Company and Member, GoshMobile Board and
> Audit Committee

JOAN F. DOESTEIN

(650) 555-5555 • Silicon City, CA • joan@joandoestein.com

Qualified Financial Expert with Tech, Financial, and Life Science Expertise

Joan Doestein is an accomplished chief financial officer and board director, with public and private company experience in the technology, financial services, and life sciences industries. She is a qualified financial expert, and has expertise in mergers and acquisitions, scaling business operations, and international expansion. Ms. Doestein has held leadership roles with companies that have shaped the course of the technology industry, such as LMNOP, Memory Block Technology, and X Networking Co, as well as emerging companies. During her career, Ms. Doestein has completed more than $X.5 billion in financings, and $X.5 billion in M&A transactions.

- Turned around the financial performance and increased the gross profit margin 250+ basis points of X Networking Company
- Led the financial due diligence and integration for the $2 billion acquisition of MegaTech Corporation
- Built a global financial shared services center, which improved quality and reduced expenses 30%.

BOARD OF DIRECTORS–AUDIT CHAIR EXPERT

GLOBAL FINANCE CO, (**[stock symbol]**), a publicly traded company that offers leasing and finance services to a worldwide customer base of [niche industry] and other commercial customers. *Independent board director,* 2017–present. *Audit committee member*, 2017–present.
PHARMACY PARTNERSHIP CO, a private subsidiary of Pharmacy Co that develops pharmaceutical products for women's health. *Independent board director,* 2015–2017. *Special committee chair and compensation committee chair,* 2016–2017. Served on special and compensation committees.
SILICON CITY CREDIT UNION, a full services credit union with $2 billion in assets. *Supervisory (audit) committee member,* 2013–2016.
FAMILY HOUSE AT SUPREME UNIVERSITY, provides support and accommodations for the families of children receiving care at Supreme University Children's Hospital. *Audit committee member*, 2008–present.

PROFESSIONAL EXPERIENCE

XYZ GROUP LLC, *President* 2010–Present
Created a management consulting business providing CFO and Strategic Advisory services for CEOs and Boards of public, and private companies. Clients engage our services to focus their company's strategy for growth, and improve financial and operational performance. Representative clients include public companies such as Circuitry Co ([stock symbol]), private equity companies in the [Name] Partner's portfolio, and privately owned companies.

X NETWORKING CO, (**[stock symbol]**) 2007–2009
Chief Financial Officer and Senior Vice President
X Networking Co is a recognized network solutions company, with $X00+ million in revenue. Led the finance, investor relations, audit, information technology, and order admin functions. Hired to turn around the company's negative trend in financial operating results.

- Turned around the financial performance of the company. Increased pro forma net income from an annual loss of ($0.04) per share to a profit of $0.09–$0.12 per share, in collaboration with the executive team.
- Increased the gross profit margin 250+ basis points. Executed major initiatives, including shifted resources to lower-cost geographies, prioritized product portfolio investments, and spearheaded cross-functional productivity programs.
- Hired a new finance and IT leadership team. Recruited over 50% of the organization's professional staff to upgrade technical skill levels and build business partnerships.

MEMORY BLOCK TECHNOLOGY, ([stock symbol]) 2004–2006
Vice-President Corporate Finance, Treasurer, and Principal Accounting Officer
Memory Block is a leader in data storage industry, with $X billion in revenue. Led the corporate controllership, FP&A, treasury, and sales and marketing business finance functions.

- Led the financial due diligence and integration for the $2 billion acquisition of MegaTech Corporation.
- Completed a $1.5 billion corporate bond offering and $2.5 billion share repurchase, to offset the share price dilution from the MegaTech acquisition.
- Built a global financial shared services center, which improved quality and reduced expenses 30%.
- Established both the initial SOX compliance process, and enterprise risk management process.

DOESTEIN GROUP, *Independent Consultant* 2001–2003
Created a management consulting business, engaged with clients and delivered services, including business strategy, business development, and interim executive management.

INTERNET INFRASTRUCTURE CORPORATION, ([stock symbol]) 2000
Vice-President and General Manager of the Search Division
Internet Infrastructure was a hypergrowth Internet infrastructure company. Hired to lead the newly formed Search Division with P&L and strategic responsibility for $75 million in revenues.
- Increased business unit revenues 118% from $34 to $75 million, through organic growth and acquisition.
- Successfully completed the $340 million acquisition of Ultimate Corporation, a subsidiary of the Mega Media Company.

LMNOP COMPANY, ([stock symbol]) 1976–2000
LMNOP is a technology industry leader in the imaging, computing, and instrumentation markets. The company grew from $2 to $42 billion in revenue, over this period.
General Manager, for an emerging software business, 1998–2000
- Built and sold an emerging communications software business for 40X the prior year's revenues.

Head of Information Technology, for the Test and Measurement business, 1992–1998
Promoted to head the information technology function for the $4 billion business. Led the 500+ person organization, located in twelve locations worldwide.
- Led the strategic planning and operational programs to develop the next-generation IT architecture, for the networked enterprise.
- Reduced operational costs ~50% and reinvested the savings into process-reengineering programs and new business applications.

Division Controller, for communications test and network test businesses, 1989–1992
Promoted through five financial positions (1976–1985), to Division Controller of the Printed
CircuitManufacturing Operation (1985–1992), to lead the Finance and IT functions for mul-
tiple product divisions.

- Collaborated with executive teams to develop strategies for growth, prioritize
  investments for new product development, and streamlined core business processes and
  systems.

EDUCATION

MASTERS IN BUSINESS ADMINISTRATION, Silicon City University, 1985
BACHELORS OF SCIENCE, Business Admin, Center State University, Central City, 1976

COMMUNITY AND PROFESSIONAL AFFILIATIONS

PROMINENT CORPORATE BOARD ASSOCIATION, Member, 2006–Present; *Cyberse-
curity Special Interest Group*, 2017–Present
WOMEN'S CORPORATE GROUP, 2017–Present
GLOBAL ASSOCIATION OF FINANCIAL EXECUTIVES, Member 2004–Present, *Silicon
Valley Chapter Board*, 2014-2015. Served on the membership committee and academic
committee.
WOMEN FOUNDERS ADVOCACY ANGELS, Investor, 2016–Present
CORPORATE GROWTH GROUP, Member 2010–2013. *Co-Chair Membership Committee*,
2010–2011.

Francis Techie CV Sample, MBA

City • Phone • email • LinkedIn • @SampleMBA

*Fintech Thought Leader, Strategy Executive, Product Executive,
and Process Innovation Executive*

C-level financial services and fintech executive and advisor who leads strategic transformation in the face of rapid technology, regulatory, and market changes. Brings a blend of consulting and corporate executive experience for industry leaders including PayForward, and HappyTime, with unique perspective on what it takes for executive teams and board of directors to define ambitious yet achievable visions and pursue organic and inorganic growth. Utilizes 25 years of experience repositioning and scaling companies through innovation, new product, market, talent, capability development, and M&A. Anticipates and identifies relevant trends, develops tangible responses, and guides companies through high stake changes–from aligning product portfolios and organizations to identifying M&A targets and integrating newly acquired companies.

- **Growth Strategy and Leadership:** Developed and presented growth strategy to the board of XXX–doubling company's market cap from $12B to $25B via an acquisition, while managing a $140M budget.

- **Revenue Driver:** Increased revenue 20% p.a. through an 88% surge in users (98M to 184M) at PayForward.

- **Agile Transformation:** Aligned a seventy-product portfolio to Agile development for HappyTime.

- **Product Strategy:** Oversaw the product suite targeted at global mid to large corporations—which accounted for $75B in transactions at BIGCard, the world's largest global payment network.

- **IPO and Board Leadership:** Prepared and was key leader in preparing HappyTime's IPO and served as member of the board of GCPS, a multinational joint venture of Commercial Card issuing banks from 2005–2007.

Expertise that Delivers Business and Board Value

Francis's expertise will benefit both legacy companies in major transition and younger companies with disruptive process innovations, in developing strategies, processes, and product launches to scale.

- Financial Technology
- Payment System
- Customer-Centric Financial Services
- Business Transformation
- Corporate Strategy
- New Market Development

Professional Experience

XYZ Inc. (North America), San Francisco, CA, *European Payment Processor, leading growth in NA.* Feb. 2017–Present
CEO

Leading the US market entry for a differentiated acquirer, issuer, and closed loop processor. Initiatives involve certifying and building out the technology and product solutions, developing the team, and leading business development and sales efforts in North America.

ABC **Technology Advisors, LLC,** San Francisco, CA 2016 to Present

Privately held consulting and advisory firm providing services to technology, financial services, and private equity companies.

FOUNDER AND MANAGING PARTNER

Advise private equity firms on payments/fintech investments (pipeline building, screening, due diligences, postinvestment strategy). Develop growth and payment strategies for technology companies. Focused on innovation, growth, and new market entry, geo expansion in areas such as payments including mobile wallets, online payments, payment acceptance, PSP/payment facilitation, B2B payments, consumer payments, healthcare payments, integrated payments, and blockchain/Bitcoin. big data, machine learning, and AI. Clients include X, W, Z.

BIGCard, *North American Merchant Acquirer* 2008–2016

CHIEF STRATEGY OFFICER

Recruited with a charter to make BIGCard more technology and product focused. Led successful corporate strategy, strategic business development, M&A, product management and development, analytics, and strategic pricing. Oversaw $250M budget and 180 employees.

- **Growth Strategy:** Developed and presented growth strategy to the board—doubling company's market cap from $15B to $30B via an acquisition.
- **Agile Transformation:** Drove successful Agile digital transformations, alignment of a seventy-product portfolio to Agile development, increasing speed and relevance of product development.
- **Product Management:** Generated greater alignment in the Product Management organization by implementing "product" as a functional discipline and consolidating six product teams from different business units and acquisitions.
- **Market Development:** Contributed to BIGCard's industry leading growth rates by executing on market development strategies, penetrating fast-growing verticals such as healthcare, specialty retail, and recurring billing.
- **Innovation:** Positioned as an innovator by initiating/leading the development of technology driven products.
- **Revenue Generator:** Increased annual revenue growth rates of > 20% by launching and guiding a portfolio of strategic initiatives such as wallet, financial hub, demand generation, identity, business services, merchant credit, consumer credit, channel strategy, shipping, and loyalty.

ABC—Palo Alto, CA 2007 to 2008

Startup business service provider of top-notch independent consultant to Fortune 1000 companies and private equity firms.

FOUNDER | WEST COAST PRACTICE LEADER | GLOBAL HEAD OF MARKETING AND COMMUNICATIONS

Cofounded ABC in 2001 and rejoined in 2007 to establish and direct the new operations for the West Coast and to lead the global marketing function.

HappyTime International 2002 to 2007

SVP, GLOBAL STRATEGY, MARKET INTELLIGENCE, AND INTERNAL CONSULTING, 2005–2007

Promoted from VP, International Strategy (2002-2004) to lead the development of strategies and executed market intelligence projects for HappyTime International's Executive Management

Team and Board of Directors. Supported the wider organization with internal consulting capabilities. Led corporate strategy, product strategies, country strategies, business plans, corporate transformation, IPO preparation, and performance enhancement. Served as key leader in preparing HappyTime's IPO. Oversaw the product suit targeted at global mid to large corporations–which accounted for $75B in transactions. Led a review of entire global product portfolio, leading to the launch of the HappyTime Signature platform and HappyTime prepaid cards product.

Consulting Firm A & Company—Germany, *Worldwide management consulting firm.* 1998 to 2002
ENGAGEMENT MANAGER (2000–2002) | **ASSOCIATE** (1998–1999)
Focused on delivering strategic business consulting services to clients in consumer goods, retail, and business services. Clients included large corporate and private equity firms and their portfolio companies.

Another Company—*Asia Division* 1991–1996
Promoted through multiple roles, including, **Divisional Controller/FP&A—Waters**, Asia region (1996), **Key Account Management,** Philippines (1995), and **Corporate Auditor** (1991–1994).

Board Experience

CLoudStore (NASDAQ: SSSS), 2014–2016. Technology company providing cloud storage of vital financial information. Key Role: Strategic advisory board member for evaluation of merger opportunities, which resulted in purchase via BigStems (NASDAQ: XXXX) and return to shareholders of 544% return over 10 years.

GoshMobile (Privately held, venture-backed company), 2010-Present. First company to offer customers option to get their daily Gosh via mobile delivery. Annual revenue: $50M. Key Roles: Audit chair, responsible for introducing sales team to key mobile venture capitalists, and global connections to companies interested in partnering.

University of Someplace, 2008–2013. Endowment trustee. Key Roles: Trusted counselor regarding selection of a new investment management firm. Led the capital campaign for new sports stadium in 2010.

Awards and Honors

Payments Executive of the Year, 2016–ABC Award Company
Fintech Women in Leadership. 2015–National Banking Council
Graduates Who Could Lead the World, 2008–Harvard Business School

Thought Leadership

A few key examples of speaking, writing, and books.

Education

International MBA–Institute for Management Development (IMD)–London School of Economics
MA, Economics and General Management–Columbia University
BA, Economics–Harvard

Personal

Marathon runner, snowboarder, softball coach for XX High School girls' team (state finals in 2018), and TEDx advisor for fintech programming.

Erika M. Cramer*

*Delivering board value through M&A, financial leadership, asset management,
and strategic investments*

San Francisco • New York • (914) 261.7775 • erika@canycap.com
• www.linkedin.com/in/erika-cramer-2034298/

Accomplished Investment Banking Executive, Advisor, and Board Member who leads corporate growth objectives and turnarounds resulting in billion-dollar outcomes through 25+ years in M&A, recapitalizations, capital raising, divestitures, succession planning, and valuations. Strong expertise in investment banking, corporate development, and building successful entrepreneurial businesses to support strategic growth initiatives, enhance competitive positioning with risk controls, and enhance shareholder value. Architect of compliance and risk management protocols, establishing and enforcing policies, procedures, and controls within highly regulated industries. Highly qualified to serve on a board seeking strategic investments, compliance oversight, asset management, and M&A knowledge.

- **M&A Leader:** Completed fifty-two transactions involving over $240B in assets under advisement/management (AUM) exchanging hands. Primarily small- to mid-sized transaction activity.
- **Fundraising Expert:** Raised over $1.5B in assets for hedge fund of funds, and single and multistrategy hedge funds. Raised several $4M+ early-stage rounds for fintech firms that required positioning while in their proof-of-concept stages, including investments made by publicly traded corporations investing from their balance sheet as the strategic "new VC investor."
- **Board Leadership:** Serves on privately held corporate board (Atlanta Life Financial Group)—served as chair of compensation committee and currently audit chair, orchestrating turnaround of reinsurance, life and P&C businesses, while leading winddown of asset management firm that held $10B in managed assets at its peak. Leading recruitment of entirely new executive leadership team and implementing succession plan, strategic relationships, product leadership through insuretech solutions, regulator relationships, and overall company transformation.
- **Broker Dealerships:** Established two registered broker dealers, one of which being a women-owned investment banking boutique.
- **Wealth Management:** Achieved trendsetting transactions, particularly in the niche area of wealth management, that withstood test of time such as Bel Air Investment Advisors sale to Fiera Capital, First Republic's purchase of Luminous Capital; permanent capital investment made by family office, Temperance Partners, and Westmount Capital (a repeat client). Active in a private family office.

Speaker: Moderated, led, and designed many M&A and financial services-focused panel discussions. Conducted a TED-style talk for the CFA Society. Has presented at several industry related conferences. Designed and organized industry events for 100 Women in Finance covering topics such as Deep Dive in Fintech, Board-Ready Women, and Sharpen Your Negotiation Process for Better Results.

Competencies That Deliver Board Value

- Domestic and Cross-Border M&A | Recapitalization
- Dispositions | Valuations
- Fund Raising

- Compliance | Risk Management
- Corporate and Employee Culture
- Succession Planning | Change Management
- Corporate Governance and Impact
- Strategy Development | Implementation
- Policy Development
- Alternative Investment Strategies
- Financial Structuring | Revenue Development
- Mentorship and Employee Compensation
- Financial Incentive Programs

Board Leadership

Atlanta Life Financial Group www.atlantalife.com 2016–Present
The only African-American insurer in the United States founded by an emancipated slave over 113 years ago

BOARD DIRECTOR | CHAIR OF AUDIT COMMITTEE OF ALFG

Brought on board for 25 years of experience in M&A and asset management to lead turnaround of this 100+ year company, which had an affiliate RIA that managed $10B AUM at its peak.

- **Crisis Management**: Involved in rebuilding an asset management firm with out-of-favor investment products by hiring new CEO and establishing an equity incentive retention program.
  - Led business wind-down as dysfunctional characteristics were bleeding into core business.
- **Turnaround:** Leading rebuild of 100+ year startup insurance company: established strategic partnership with AON to leverage AON's client base and product development with Atlanta Life's great heritage and diversity status.
  - Building and implementing strategy to expand products and risk management services as a diversity supplier of group life reinsurance and property and casualty products with Fortune 500 companies and leading insurance carriers.
- **Succession Planning**: Led terminating old guard and rebuilding C-suite, and statutory and advisory boards—wrote advisory board charter.
- **Product Leadership**: Implemented strategy for new product development with cybersecurity, active shooter, and green insurance products.
- **Company Transformation**: Leads interim active role as the company reemerges with stronger policies, procedures, financial accountability, client relationships, and strategy implementation.
- **Shareholder Communication**: Established transparent communication with shareholders, regulators and other stakeholders presenting challenges, opportunities, goals, and plan for implementation.

Trips for Kids, Marin Chapter, www.tripsforkidsmarin.org 2016–Present *California 501(c) (3) nonprofit with mission to provide transformative cycle cycling experiences for underserved youth.*

DIRECTOR

Serves as director for the Marin Chapter, which expanded to operating in around seventy-five locations throughout the United States, Canada, Israel, and Sierra Leone. TFK has opened the world of cycling to over 145,000 youth and worked with over 400 local agencies and organizations.

- **Change Management and Compensation:** Vetted and led interview process for the hiring of national executive director; hired and developed a compensation plan for new event planner.

Event Planning: Cochaired the 30th Anniversary Event Planning.

- **Funding Leader:** Actively solicited corporate sponsorship and donations.

Professional Experience

CANY Capital, LLC. 2018–present *Family office for the management of board directorships and family-owned investments. CANY is the sister company to Alternative Access Capital, LLC.*
PARTNER Leads setting up wealth management strategies, reporting systems, and establishing multi-generational governance tools for personal family practice of board directorships. Sourcing and analyzing investment opportunities as well as selecting external wealth managers and advisors.

Silver Lane Advisors LLC. 2007–2017 *Investment banking boutique specializing in strategic advisory services for asset management, wealth advisory, and fintech sectors.*

ADVISORY DIRECTOR | FORMER MANAGING DIRECTOR, PARTNER, AND CHIEF COMPLIANCE OFFICER

Managed team in successfully advising, structuring, and negotiating over 30 transactions, collectively representing more than $200B in managed assets. Represented founding owners, executive management and boards in executing strategic initiatives. Involved in all aspects of managing a registered broker/dealer, including human resources, office management, marketing, legal, compliance, public relations, technology, and financial management.

- **Growth:** With partner, grew the firm from two employees and zero revenues to 10 professionals, including five managing directors, and a recurring revenue stream on average between $5M and $10M annually.
  - Received numerous accolades and awards, earning a reputation as the "go-to investment bank for wealth management M&A."
- **M&A Leader:** Sourced, managed, and processed fifty-two transactions over career and built a firm that at any time processed between ten and fifteen active mandates.
- **Governance**: Served as the chief compliance officer and a partner–developed all written policies and procedures for purposes of FINRA and the SEC. Developed employee manuals, training program, new client commitment committee, employee reviews, and hiring, firing, and mentoring.
- **Business Expansion:** Opened new business branch in San Francisco, expanding client service and business development.

Alternative Access Capital, LLC 2003–2007 *Private placement firm specializing in raising capital for alternative investment strategies.*

PARTNER

Established broker dealer specializing in raising institutional capital for asset management firms selling alternative investment strategies.

- **Fundraising Expert**: Raised over $1.5B in assets for hedge fund of funds, single and multistrategy hedge funds.

U.S. Trust Company of NY (Formerly a subsidiary of Charles Schwab Corp.) 2001–2003

SENIOR VICE PRESIDENT, STRATEGIC DEVELOPMENT

Reported to the CEO and president, set forth a national expansion strategy, integrated acquired entities and acted as liaison with parent company's corporate development team. Project management for implementation of bank policies and procedures.

Berkshire Capital Securities, LLC. 1990–2001 *Investment bank specializing in M&A in financial services industry.*

DIRECTOR & PARTNER

Advised on twenty-eight completed transactions involving analytics, deal sourcing, and deal processing for a firm that grew from six to thirty employees over tenure.

Education and Certifications

MBA, Finance, Pace University | **BA, Finance,** West Virginia University
Certified: Series 79, 7, 63, and 24 **Professional Affiliations**
COMMITTEE MEMBER, Angel, 100 Women in Finance, for the Northern CA Chapter
MEMBER, National Association of Corporate Directors
MEMBER, Athena Alliance
FORMER COMMITTEE MEMBER, Coalition for Preemie Development; public advocate and supporter for The March of Dimes

Personal Interests

Triathlete | Marathoner | Avid Cyclist
Wife and mother of two daughters
Working Spanish language; enjoy studying world cultures and travel

---

* Erika M. Cramer's board biography has not been deidentified.

Natalie E. Superstar

Unique ability to identify customer, technology, and market insight to drive strategy

Beautiful Town, MA • Mobile: 123-456-7890 • Email: natalie.superstar@gmail.com
• www.linkedin.com/in/nataliesuperstar

INSIGHTFUL TECHNOLOGY EXECUTIVE AND BOARD MEMBER WHO BUILDS SHAREHOLDER VALUE

Executive and board member with extensive technology experience and significant leadership accomplishments in B2B. Ability to synthesize complex data and integrate customer and technology insight to design business strategy and grow shareholder value. Well-developed diplomatic skills and natural collaborator bringing diverse teams together to solve problems.

- Insight. Identified the complexity of deploying network security as an underserved customer pain point, and built strategy, innovative policy management, open APIs and marketing narrative to focus, and drive business results.
- Growth. Identified missed market opportunity, and redirected and redefined products that grew data center switching business ##X in # years to $###M.
- Strategy. Collaborated on the creation of a #-year multihorizon strategy for business transformation and growth for the board of directors.
- Financial management. Reviewed and approved strategic priorities, annual budgets and forecasts. Presented quarterly financial results and quarterly forecasts. Communicated strategy and differentiation to financial industry analysts.
- Contract negotiations and alliances. Negotiated OEM, licensing, and vendor agreements across a broad range of technologies and businesses. Initiated and managed relationships with alliance partners including Brand Company A, Brand Company B, and Brand Company C, among others.
- Governance and cross-team leadership. Ran regulatory compliance governance committee in healthcare. Brought together a diverse team from siloed divisions to achieve challenging objectives.

EXECUTIVE CAREER

Software startup innovating enterprise IT infrastructure for data-intensive computing
Chief Product Officer

- Brought in to lead company strategy, product definition, positioning and narrative
- Identified the ability for users to "create their own servers" as the key technology insight, and retargeted sales and marketing to customer segments where IT is typically defined as do-it-yourself type masters of their infrastructure

Amazing Company A, Beautiful City, MA
20XX–Present
ADVISOR, Beautiful City, MA
Advisor and mentor to early-stage technology company founders and boards
Amazing Company B, Beautiful City, MA $#B networking and cybersecurity company
Senior Vice President, Product Management, Strategy and Partnerships
20XX–Present

- Recruited to lead $# billion cloud services, cybersecurity, and networking portfolios; engaged with financial analysts, customers, media, and partners
- Grew data center switching business from $##M to $###M and overall switching revenue to $#B
- Launched cloud-based machine learning XXXXXXX service
- Met with board members regarding company business, strategy, and technology
- Led quarterly business reviews to CEO staff to present financial results and provide context to revenue, margin and profitability regarding customers, competitors, trends, and technology
- Reviewed and analyzed acquisitions and investments as well as partnership agreements
- Built customer relationships with Brand Company A, Brand Company B, and Company C, Brand Company D, and Brand Company E, among others

XXXXXXX NATIONAL ASSOCIATION, Beautiful City, TN

Board Member, Board of Directors
- Board director with Iconic Company A, Iconic Company B, and Iconic Company C, Iconic Company D, and Iconic Company E's and other Fortune 500 executives to define membership education, grow membership, evolve industry standards and regulations, and share learnings

Amazing Company C, Beautiful City, MA 20XX–20XX $## billion science-led global healthcare company

Head of Omnichannel Customer Engagement, North America

- Recruited to lead company strategy and transformation to digital
- Engaged the CEO and executive staff to align strategy and execution across siloed divisions
- Created company's first cross-divisional team to develop a global framework and digital shared service to deliver digital content and marketing campaigns
- Led compliance committee to oversee and manage regulatory impacts to digital health

Amazing Company D, Beautiful City, MA 20XX–20XX Marketing and business strategy advisory for the transformation to digital business

Advisor

- Worked with executives at Fortune 1000 companies including Brand Company A, Brand Company B, and Company C, Brand Company D, and Brand Company E, and early-stage startups including Company A, Company B, and Company C

Award-Winning Author

- Expert on the rise of social media. Authored Great Book (20XX)
- Received accolades from Iconic Company's CEO/Founder; won Book Award A and Book Award B

Amazing Company E, Beautiful City, MA

Early-stage software company that offered highly scalable, reliable data storage

President, Chief Executive Officer, and Board Director

20XX–20XX

- Brought in by the Board of Directors to lead, operate, and manage the company
- Defined strategy and innovative product direction; secured bridge funding

- Led early customer adoption with Brand Company A, Brand Company B, and Company C, Brand Company D, and Brand Company E; developed relationships with Brand Company A, Brand Company B, and Company C, Brand Company D, and Brand Company E for technology licensing

EDUCATION

MBA, Great University, XXXXX School of Business and Management, Beautiful City, SC BA, Amazing University, Beautiful City, LA

APPENDIX F

Board Biography and CV Templates

Use this worksheet to build a first draft of your own board biography. Of course, some sections may need to be modified or removed to fit your purposes. And you may choose to add sections as needed. Your career, skills, experience, and expertise are unique, and your board biography will be as well. Once you have this worksheet completed, feel free to format and edit as you wish. As you can see from Appendix E, there is no one "right" way for a board biography to look. Overall, focus on conveying your unique value as a prospective director. Finally, this appendix also includes a list of jargon words to avoid for board papers and recommends better words to use instead.

Board Biography Template

Written in narrative

[NAME]

City, LinkedIn, phone, email, professional @twitter,
professional website

Tagline that highlights your wheelhouse

[INSERT NAME] begins with a paragraph or two that includes your profile statement (see samples). Include a theme to your overall leadership career accomplishments including key high-level executive titles and for-profit board service. Explain industries (e.g., consumer electronics,) where you have expertise. Types or stages of companies where your experiences have been earned (e.g., (B2B, SaaS) public companies, startups, rapid growth, turnaround). What is your reputation for successful accomplishments (e.g., she grows, she turns around, and she launches)? What kind of boards will your experiences be helpful for (e.g., she is well suited to bring her public company CFO experience into a small public or pre-IPO tech company)?

Paragraphs related to your for-profit board experiences are excellent to add. These can be both positions as a board member and your interactions with a corporate board in your executive roles.

Paragraph(s) outlining executive positions. Focus on explaining transitions from position to position. Highlight skills gained from experiences and how you have used them in subsequent experiences. Also highlight quantifiable accomplishments (e.g., revenue, number of employees, number of offices, products, and regulatory challenges).

Highlight specific examples of strategic, operational, and/or financial expertise. This is where you will emphasize the value you can bring to a board.

Brief highlight of nonprofit board services should include positions such as audit committee or a major governance issues you have addressed. Include honors that you have received and how you might be classified as a thought leader by noting where you speak or are seen as an expert.

[INSERT NAME] earned a BA in [Major and any honors] from [University name] and has earned a [higher degree name] from [University name]. She has also earned the [list certificates such as CIPP/US]

An optional addition can be a short sentence that shows something interesting about you personally, such as you run marathons, enjoy flying glider planes, or have a low golf handicap.

Board Resume/CV Template

[NAME]

City, LinkedIn, phone, email, professional @twitter, professional website

Tagline that highlights your wheelhouse (same as bio)

Paragraphs detailing your value proposition with key titles, key companies, key wheelhouse expertise with overall approach on how you have been a steward of the companies for whom you have held leadership positions. Summarizes the bio.

- Expertise 1—accomplishment which moved the needle for Company X with an outcome with key metrics
- Expertise 2—accomplishment which moved the needle for Company X with an outcome with key metrics
- Expertise 3—accomplishment which moved the needle for Company X with an outcome with key metrics
- Expertise 4—accomplishment which moved the needle for Company X with an outcome with key metrics
- Expertise 5—accomplishment which moved the needle for Company X with an outcome with key metrics

Expertise that Delivers Business and Board Value

NAME's expertise will benefit companies .... target the types of companies most likely to benefit from your expertise—if possible, without narrowing too much.

MATRIX of Skills/Expertise—8 max

Skill 1 (e.g., Talent Management) Skill 2! Skill 3
Expertise 1 (e.g., M&A) Expertise 2! Expertise 3

Professional Experience

Inc., San Francisco, CA Dates XXXXX

TITLE

Overview of company and key scope of areas under your leadership.

- Accomplishment
- Accomplishment
- Accomplishment

Inc.2, San Francisco, CA Dates XXXXX
TITLE

Overview of company and key scope of areas under your leadership.

- Accomplishment
- Accomplishment
- Accomplishment

Board Experience (in this order)

Company name, type of company (public, private), size, years of service. Key accomplishments, committee assignments

Corporate Boards
Advisory Boards
Nonprofit boards
Board Training and Certification
Presentations in corporate boardroom

Awards and Honors

Key examples

Thought Leadership

Key examples of speaking, writing, and books

Education

MBA—University of ZZZ, Date M.A. with Honors, University of XXX, Date
B.A., Economics—X College, Date

Personal

2 lines of personal memorable items

Words For Board Documents

"I've seen so many board documents that have trite words that don't show the impact the person had on a company's bottom or top line. As a senior executive, your goal in your board documents is to have statements that display leadership and end-results. Words do matter!"

—Nancy Sheppard, Board Candidate Consultant, Women2Boards and the Athena Alliance

Worst Jargon Words

- Best of breed
- Go-getter
- Responsible for (what you accomplished instead)
- Thinks outside the box
- Synergy
- Go-to-person
- Thought leadership (unless very specific and proven by examples)
- Value add
- Results-driven
- Team player
- Hard worker
- Strategic thinker
- Dynamic
- Self-motivated
- Detail oriented
- Proactive
- Track record

Better Words

- Achieves
- Improves
- Manages
- Trains/mentors
- Creates
- Resolves
- Authors
- Volunteers
- Influences
- Increases/decreases
- Ideas
- Negotiates
- Launched
- Revenue/profits
- Under budget
- Won
- Grew
- Scaled

About the Author

Olga V. Mack is a powerhouse: She is a corporate governance guru, blockchain strategist, startup advisor, nationally recognized author, public speaker, award-winning general counsel, and women's advocate. Olga earned both her BA and JD from UC Berkeley. She has received Watermark Make Your Mark, Corporate Counsel of the Year, Women Leaders in Technology Law, and numerous other awards. Olga is very involved in her community and serves on numerous boards and advisory boards. She is also a passionate women's advocate. She founded the Women Serve on Boards movement (**womenserveonboards.com**) to achieve gender parity on corporate boards in her lifetime.

About the Contributor

Nancy Sheppard is passionate about helping to lead the movement to have more qualified women have a seat at the board table. She founded Women2Boards as a way to assist both corporate boards and women connect and improve gender diversity in the boardroom. She joined The Athena Alliance in 2017 as part of their leadership team to continue this mission. She advises women on the path to the boardroom, speaks on the subject nationally, and works with corporate boards that want to find talented individuals for their boardroom (who happen to be women).

Nancy has 30+ years of management and governance experience in banking associations; financial services industry; and legislative, regulatory, and political environments. She was the CEO of Western Independent Bankers, the largest regional banking association in the United States, for over 20 years. She served on two private company boards for financial institution products, created educational programs for directors and senior executives, and worked with hundreds of banks' CEOs and board members.

Index

OTHER TITLES IN THE ENTREPRENEURSHIP AND SMALL BUSINESS MANAGEMENT COLLECTION

Scott Shane, Case Western University, *Editor*

- *Navigating Entrepreneurship: 11 Proven Keys to Success* by Larry Jacobson
- *Global Women in the Start-up World: Conversations in Silicon Valley* by Marta Zucker
- *Understanding the Family Business: Exploring the Differences Between Family and Nonfamily Businesses, Second Edition* by Keanon J. Alderson
- *Growth-Oriented Entrepreneurship* by Alan S. Gutterman
- *Founders* by Alan S. Gutterman
- *Entrepreneurship* by Alan S. Gutterman
- *Sustainable Entrepreneurship* by Alan S. Gutterman
- *Startup Strategy Humor: Democratizing Startup Strategy* by Rajesh K. Pillania
- *The Leadership Development Journey: How Entrepreneurs Develop Leadership Through Their Lifetime* by Jen Vuhuong
- *Getting to Market With Your MVP: How to Achieve Small Business and Entrepreneur Success* by J.C. Baker
- *Can You Run Your Business With Blood, Sweat, and Tears? Volume I: Blood* by Stephen Elkins-Jarrett and Nick Skinner
- *Can You Run Your Business With Blood, Sweat, and Tears? Volume II: Sweat* by Stephen Elkins-Jarrett and Nick Skinner
- *Can You Run Your Business With Blood, Sweat, and Tears? Volume III: Tear* by Stephen Elkins-Jarrett and Nick Skinner
- *Family Business Governance: Increasing Business Effectiveness and Professionalism* by Keanon J. Alderson
- *Department of Startup: Why Every Fortune 500 Should Have One* by Ivan Yong Wei Kit and Sam Lee
- *From Vision to Decision: A Self-Coaching Guide to Starting a New Business* by Dana K. Dwyer

Announcing the Business Expert Press Digital Library

Concise e-books business students need for classroom and research

This book can also be purchased in an e-book collection by your library as

- a one-time purchase,
- that is owned forever,
- allows for simultaneous readers,
- has no restrictions on printing, and
- can be downloaded as PDFs from within the library community.

Our digital library collections are a great solution to beat the rising cost of textbooks. E-books can be loaded into their course management systems or onto students' e-book readers.

The **Business Expert Press** digital libraries are very affordable, with no obligation to buy in future years. For more information, please visit **www.businessexpertpress.com/librarians**. To set up a trial in the United States, please email **sales@businessexpertpress.com**.

CPSIA information can be obtained
at www.ICGtesting.com
Printed in the USA
FSHW021636151219

9 781949 991406